URBAN REDEVELOPMENT
A Study of High-Rise Buildings

The Author

Dr. K. Narayan Reddy (*b.* 1955), presently working in the Department of Geography, Osmania University, has been actively engaged in research and teaching after completing his studies at Osmania University. He was closely associated with a number of research studies in the department. He conducted many field studies and guided students in their project works. He has presented many research papers in the national conferences. Dr. Reddy is the author of many research articles and reports. His field of interest is Urban Studies.

URBAN REDEVELOPMENT
A Study of High-Rise Buildings

K. NARAYAN REDDY
Department of Geography
Osmania University
Hyderabad

Foreword by
PROF. N. BALAKRISHNA REDDY
Vice-Chairman, Council of Higher Education
Govt. of Andhra Pradesh

CONCEPT PUBLISHING COMPANY, NEW DELHI - 110059

ISBN 81-7022-531-0

First Published 1996

Published and Printed by
Ashok Kumar Mittal
Concept Publishing Company
A/15-16, Commercial Block, Mohan Garden
New Delhi-110059 (India)
Phones : 5554042, 5504042

FOREWORD

Urban redevelopment especially in old cities is of paramount importance. The author deserves compliments for taking up his research on this theme. Urban crisis is the result of urban decay. Urban redevelopment porports to mitigate the process of urban deterioration, decay and decadence. Most of our old cities are loosing the structural and functional value especially in their central parts as a result of decay of old structures and insufficient infrastrctural facilities. Redevelopment of these old structures is indeed a task and it involves a continuous process which needs to be pursued with renewed vigour.

High-rise and high-density developments are the result of growing demand for space in the central parts of cities and it appears that this is the only rational way of redevelopment that could be adopted. The neglect of central or inner areas of major cities had an adverse impact on their physical and socio-economic scenario. A comprehensive redevelopment and improvement is not only necessary but also becomes inevitable. By and large, redevelopment is taking place in the inner parts of our cities in the form of vertical growth as there is no scope for horizontal extension and expansion.

Single residencial entities in the form of independent houses with individual boundaries and compound walls occupy a large chunk of land in the form of open space around buildings which cannot be availed for community use. In the case of high- rise development, the land coverage of the building itself is less while at the same time the open spaces are put to the community use. Another advantage of high-rise development is reduction in the cost of development of new sites as the utility services are common. The rise in revenues from taxes is also an added advantage. It is universally accepted now that vertical growth of structures alone provides rational solution to the urban housing problem in large cities. It also provides an answer to the prohibitive exhorbitant cost of land in cities.

The role of multi-storeyed buildings in urban habitat and its interaction with urban systems is multi-dimensional. Social problems arising out of this new development should be looked into properly. Particularly, the nature of family relationships, degree of statisfaction and family security, environmental and psychological effects, adverse effects of failure of water, power, sewarge systems at times etc. need be studied carefully. Any new pattern and plan of development should create a satisfactory and healthy social environment.

The present study is made in a sequential order covering all aspects of high-rise development as a redevelopment process. The role of private entrepreneurs and government agencies in the promotion of high-rise housing industry is carefully analysed and explained. The commercial and business use of high-rise space is examined from different perspectives. The problems faced by the high-rise dwellers are examined in an exhaustive manner so as to help the planners to provide better facilities in the future developments ensuring that the same problems do not recur. A socio-economic analysis of the residents in high-rise buildings provides a clear canvas on which their social structure and requirements could be silhouetted. The author made an earnest endeavour to study the environmental implications of the high-rise redevelopment. In this context, a study of micro-climatic changes, heat islands, greenhouse effect and such other issues are very relevant.

This profound research work carried out by Dr. Narayan Reddy has provided a good insight into the contemporary problems and perspectives of redevelopment in old cities in general and Hyderabad—Secunderabad city in particular. I am sure that scholars, planners, researchers and government will evince keen interest in this good piece of research work. I am also sure that this will stimulate and encourage many others to take up more such works.

Hyderabad,
Dt. 19-09-93.

N. Balakrishna Reddy

ACKNOWLEDGEMENT

I express my deep sense of gratitude to Prof. K.N. Gopi, my research guide for his unstinted support and encouragement throughout the research period. I am extremely grateful to Prof. K. Vithal Reddy who inspired me to undertake this research work. I am thankful to Prof. R.Ram Mohan Rao for providing all facilities and extending the assistance needed by me.

I am grateful to Mr. N. Krishna Murthy for extending his help during the field survey. My thanks are due to Mr. Y.R.B. Sharma for his Computer assistance in the processing of questionnaires. Particular thanks are due to Dr. P. Padmanabha Rao for his excellent Cartographic support and Computer graphics.

I feel pleasure to record my sense of gratitude to all the Faculty members of the Department of Geography for their friendly suggestions and encouragement for this research work. My thanks must also go to all the persons in charge in various offices for rendering their valuable help in the data collection. I also thank all the individuals who responded generously to the questionnaires and participated in the discussions.

My heart felt thanks are due to my friend and colleague Mr. B. Damodar who took keen interest in Typing the manuscript and extending accurate Typing services. Many individuals and institutions have extended co-operation and assistnace to me and I am grateful to one and all.

K. Narayan Reddy

CONTENTS

LIST OF FIGURES

LIST OF TABLES

1

INTRODUCTION

Conceptual Framework

The cities due to their faster growth and long history tend to change their structural pattern to overcome the deterioration, and dilapidation as measure of checking their decay. Redevelopment process takes place to keep up the life of the city and to activate further development in the new dimension. Urban places with long history may loose their structural, functional and economic value in the central parts as result of decay of old structures and insufficient infrastructural facilities. These old structures are not able to meet the demands of increasing functions. It necessitates the remodelling or redevelopment of the existing old structures to accommodate the growing needs of the commercial and residential use.

The recent past has seen some genuine changes and growing realisation that Urban Renewal and Redevelopment of the central parts are inevitable. The terms 'Urban Renewal' and 'Redevelopment' to be considered as a continuous process. It includes the technical real estate operations of assembling sizeable tracts of land in built-up blighted areas and clearing off the present buildings, and putting up new structures which create more build-up space in a healthy environment. Actually the redevelopment process has been going on continuously in almost every parts of the inner cities. As cities grow, the residential areas replace farms, business districts replace residential areas and factories and office buildings replace shops.[1] Generally these changes have been in response to demands for more intensive land use. For the most part, the redevelopment that has taken place has been sporadic, unorganized, and without reference to any comprehensive plan of community development.

Urban Redevelopment and Urban Renewal—Distinguished and Defined.

The process of restoring the badly deteriorated areas of cities to properly planned and economically sound conditions and the actions which are taken to arrest the process of urban decay are designated by the terms 'Urban Redevelopment' and 'Urban Renewal'. A clear distinction between the two terms is not made so far. As per the earlier studies in the field, urban redevelopment has been defined broadly - "as those policies, and activities that would do away with the major forms of physical blight in cities and bring about changes in urban sturcture and institutions contributing to a favourable environment for a healthy civic, economic, and social life for all urban dwellers.[2]

Urban Redevelopment which comes within the scope of the renewal concept is used to describe as any replacement of old structures with new ones. It is also thought of as synonymous with slum clearance and rehousing. The term, however, is much broader and may involve complete redevelopment of areas for commerce, industry, transport, institutional or public recreation, and other purposes without any reference to housing also. Likewise urban redevelopment may be concerned with rehabilitation or development of open spaces as in the case of dead or arrested sub-divisions where no slum clearance or demolition of any kind is involved. By common usage and accepted meaning, urban redevelopment has come to be applied more specifically to any organized effort by a public authority directed to be task of reclaiming or restoring any deteriorated area of substantial size which, under existing conditions, cannot be carried out by the individual owners.[3]

Most of the times the term 'Redevelopment' is used interchangeably with renewal, rehabilitation and conservation and clearnace. In fact they may be distinguished from one another in terms of their genesis, planning, execution and funding and so on.

Clearance is the demolition or removal of all or nearly all of the buildings from an area, often accompanied by a new site layout and underground utilities. On the other hand the urban conservation means measures to maintain or to improve the quality of residential districts without extensive clearance. It is a process of recycling urban property and environment to a new use, re-use or proper use without significant alteration in the art and architecture. Maximum care is taken to retain the original architectural uniqueness. It is closely related to rehabilitation in the process of change but in rehabilitation, the structure is accommodated through alterations and repairs to fit in the new environment and to meet the changing socio-economic needs. Whereas, redevelopment presupposes the demolition of the structure and its replacement by a new one. Fresh planning and execution is involved in this process.

Urban renewal is of more recent origin and includes within its scope the concept of urban redevelopment, conservation and rehabilitation. However, these terms have come to get a rather specific meaning, but not entirely replaced by the coinage of the broader term of urban renewal.

The concept of urban renewal is a more modern and comprehensive method of combating urban blight than urban redevelopment. It is a process by which a large area of a town slowly renews itself and changes its character to fit in with the new socio-economic needs. As Gordon E. Cherry characterised, the urban renewal is "a highly complex process of economic, technological and social change sometimes guided, sometimes constrained by public intervention".[4]

Scott Greer observes that the basic aim of urban renewal is the maintenance and improvement of the existing housing stock.[5] It is a blueprint for social action for checking the slum and blight in the cities. Werner Hirsch conceives the urban renewal as a method by which down town areas could be rescued from blight. He also points out that one of its major side effect may actually be to increase the rate of degradation of remaining structures in the city, as well as to raise the price of low-quality housing.

Urban renewal is aimed at preventing the spread of blight and rehabilitating affected areas through measures short of clearance. Measures employed under urban renewal, in strict sense, are not a part of urban redevelopment and include such steps as the enactment and enforcement of housing, health and safety standards, the encouragement of building maintenance and repair and the rehabilitation of buildings which are still structurally sound and have economic value. Urban renewal is thus aimed not only at clearing our urban communities of slums and blighted areas but also at eliminating the causes of slums and blight.

Every urban renewal programme that is undertaken should be based on comprehensive plan of the community. As the clearance of slums, the removal of blight and elimination of their causes are the primary objectives of urban renewal, the Renewal Plan should be a comprehensive plan with environmental, social and economic connotations. Therefore, essentially the renewal programme has become a public responsibility although the private agencies are involved in its implementation.

Blight and Slums

Blight, blighted area and slums are the terms which are closely associated with the urban redevelopment and renewal. It is commonly said that the objective of redevelopment is to do away with urban blight. Blight is a general or a generic term. It never applied to a single building, usually refers to an area. It also refers to no one characteristic or condition nor even to any one set of conditions or characteristics that are always found in the same combination. It is commonly agreed that the two basic characteristics of blighted areas are substandardness and either stagnation or deterioration.[6]

Blight does not stand still, it has a way of spreading from house to house, from block to block, from neighbourhood to neighbourhood. Blight can be arrested provided it is caught early enough. Once it reached an advanced stage of deterioration, the clearance and redevelopment only will solve it.

On the other hand the slum is blighted area with poor amenities, inhabited by low income population and insecure family life. Various people have defined slum in different ways. According to Gouder, the slum is an environment that lacks the basic amenities of good living condition and is regarded as the worst form of human habitations. Slum is substandard social organization with full of chaos and confusion. Most of the slums face the problems of water supply, electricity, ineffective drainage facilities and inefficient circulation system. The remedy for the slum improvement lies in the renewal programme. Scott Greer observes that a slum or blighted area is for purposes of urban renewal, an areally concentrated collection of substandard dwellings.

Though slums and blight seem to be identical, they differ in some respects. Slums are merely residential blight. The meaning of blight applies to the areas other than the residential also, commercial and industrial districts - the two major types of non residential areas - are the examples that meet the criterial of substandardness and stagnation of deterioration. Complex forms of blight are said to exist when an area contains a mixture of incompatible landuses, obsolete or impractical layout of plots, blocks and streets, unsafe and unhealthful conditions are existing.[7]

Blight results from a complexity of inter-related physical, economic and social forces and conditions. It is due to either neglect or to inadequacy in original construction of the buildings also. If buildings are poorly constructed or improperly designed their utility is greatly diminished. Neglect and improper maintenance leads to the creaping in blight over a wide area. Blighted area is one which is an economic liability to the civic authorities.

Planning objectives and Effects of Redevelopment.

If the renewal or redevelopment programme is intended for an area, it should be based upon a comprehensive development plan of the community. The primary objectives of urban renewal and redevelopment are clearance of slums, the removal of blight and the elimination of their causes. In areas where clearance is required, the redevelopment should be based upon the most appropriate landuse for the area as established by the comprehensive plan. Unfortuantely in our cities the development process is taking place in a sporadic and piecemeal basis that too mostly in the central parts of the city where intensive landuse is resulted, by means of its growing demand and importance. This unplanned development may sometimes accrue benefits and also strains the surroundings. However, immediate result of redevelopment of an area leads to rise in revenues from taxes. There may also be a reduction in the costs of many service operations. The raising of social and physical standards in the neighbourhood produces the real advantage.

Generally in Indian cities the redevelopment process accelerates at the instances of private developers. In Urban renewal programmes, where redevelopment is required, the tasks involved are ordinarily beyond the resources of private individuals. Even if the private developer has the financial means, he has to normally face the difficulties in acquiring all the land because of the diversity of ownership. The refusal of owners to sell, and the tax situation of the property will lodge him in great difficulty. A successful redevelopment programme can be carried out only where all the properties subject to redevelopment are assembled under one ownership. Urban redevelopment is justified by the fact that a community liability will be removed and that these will enhance the community asset. This is of vital concern to the city as a whole which benefits from the higher tax base and the lowered costs of functional services. Urban redevelopment has also been criticised as it is not providing a solution to the housing needs of persons of low incomes as most of the displaced persons would not be in a position to live in rebuilt areas. In the Indian cities, most of the lower income groups of population live in obsolescent second-hand dwellings, and that as structures are reduced by demolition the occupants may have a decreasing chance of finding accommodations which they can afford. The built-up outlying areas will provide housing for those people who are displaced with the consequence of inner city redevelopment.

Redevelopment in CBD

Generally redevelopment takes place first in the central parts of the city where the demand for commercial and residential use is more. The land values also reach its peak in these areas. In anticipation of high rentals renovation of CBD takes place. Aged and deteriorated old structures, which produce less financial returns are removed and redeveloped as commercial facilities, office buildings or expensive high-rise apartments.

The intensified commercial redevelopment necessitates the vertical growth of the building structures. The nearby substandard areas also tend to change their morphology. The financial returns from the buildings are more in and around the heart of the city. High density of population also inculcates the tallness of the buildings in the central areas. Redevelopment by demolition of old buildings is the only way as one can hardly find the vacant lands in these areas. The process may not reduce the pressure in these areas, but on the other it increases the burden on both services and functions.

Historical Perspective

The concept of urban redevelopment is of a recent origin and in India it is still in the infant stage. The term involves in rejuvanating the urban areas where such areas are in the process of degeneration or decline due to a variety of factors. Rebuilding of the inner parts is essential as the deterioration and decay has set in with obsolescence of the cities. Slums and blighted areas have to be elimiated to bring in a healthy environment and social organisation.

Redevelopment was first attempted in the U.K. and U.S.A. In the form of a federal programme the redevelopment of urban areas as a planning requirement, enacted by the U.S.A. government in Housing Act of 1949. The programme was first started with New York city for the redevelopment of its inner areas. In 1955, the Housing Act of U.S.A. converted slum clearance and redevelopment to urban renewal and made possible the creation of an urban renewal administration. The concept was further extended by the Housing Act of 1959. Community Renewal Programmes were undertaken with the help of federal funds. Although the problem has been recognised officially in U. K. earlier, it was not until the 1930s the modern process of slum clearance and urban redevelopment programme was evolved formally. Under section 25 of the Housing Act of 1930, it was included in the local authority programmes. Since then with necessary alterations the redevelopment process of the urban areas was continuously implemented as a public responsibility. This was felt seriously in other European countries also after Second World War. The first two decades following the Second World War witnessed urban transformation on a considerable scale in the developed countries.

The concept of urban renewal and redevelopment in India can be traced to the year 1965 when the committee on urban land policy of the Ministry of Health, Government of India mooted urban renewal to tackle the programme of congestions and overcrowded areas. It considered three alternatives, viz., (i) wholesale demolitions and thorough redevelopment, (ii) selective urban renewal, and (iii) gradual improvement. The process of wholesale demolition and thorough redevelopment was rejected outright and the gradual improvement is approved cosidering the financial and social implications. The committee also envisaged the role of the local bodies in evolving a systematic policy of longterm redevelopment schemes. The recommendations of the committee had been followed by few local bodies of the metropolitân cities in a piecemeal manner. However, the redevelopment process in the Indian cities was a sporadic and gradual development. A schematic representation of redevelopment process is shown in Fig. 1.1.

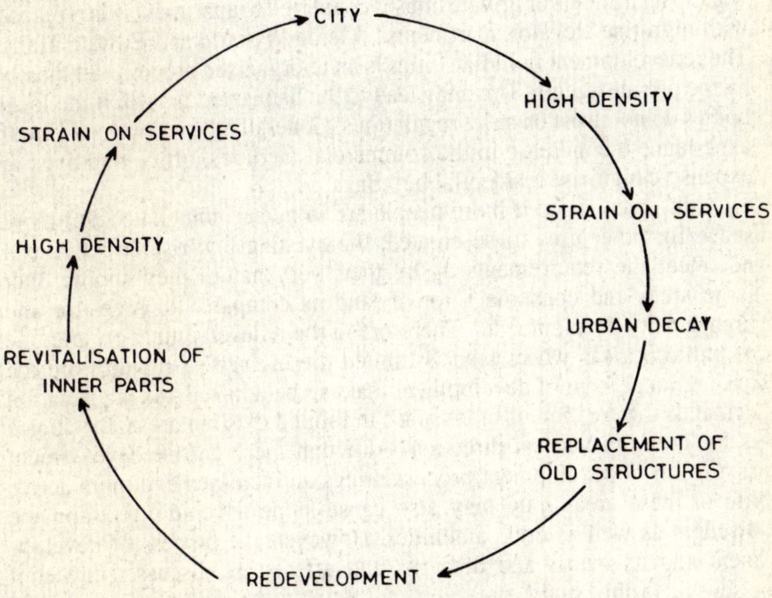

Fig. 1.1 : Urban Redevelopment Process (Schematic)

Urban Redevelopment and High-rise Buildings

The development of High-rise buildings follows closely the growth of the city. They are a natural response to dense population concentrations, scarcity of land, and high land costs. The functions in the central city grows rapidly as the main requirements for a place to live and place to work increase with bulging of population in the city. Unfortunately the land available to keep pace with man's needs is strictly limited and somemtimes prohibitively expensive. Many urban areas in India have already reached the limits of horizontal growth and as a result the only alternative left is vertical development. The age and deterioration of structures produce lack of financial profitability. Generally in the central areas of the city the demand is growing and people who can afford high rentals and construction costs try to locate their business and residences in these areas. Residential deterioration does not affect commercial development seriously in these areas but as the result of high demand the commercial redevelopment inculcates the residential development and because of the space problem vertical development takes place slowly. In many inner-city neighbourhoods of North America and Europe redevelopment, most often, means that "dilapidated housing - mainly walkup apartments or private houses converted to apartments - is replaced with high-rise elevator apartments" (Gerda Wekarle and Edward Hall). The redevelopment in Indian cities is an unorganised process and mostly by the private agents. This may lead to the haphazard growth if the local bodies do not insist on strict regulations. Generally the redeveloped areas experience the increase in the commercial facilities, office buildings or expensive high-rise residential buildings.

In given space if more people are to be accommodated and more space for other uses to be created, the existing low rise structure can not meet the requirements as by their very nature they sprawl over large areas and consume a lot of land as compared to high-rise and high density developments. Therefore in the redevelopment programme of built-up areas where land is limited the high-rise structures are the only rational form of development that can be adopted. As the situation demands the creation of more space in limited existing areas, the choice is for going in vertical direction. Although the high-rise development as a result of development process brings an increased and more active life in these areas they may also cause some adverse effects on the dwellers as well as civic amenities. However, the process of development and its mertis and demerits and effects are discussed in detail elsewere in this study.

Urban Redevelopment : Retrospective

The various aspects of urban renewal and redevelopment has been studied in depth in the developed countries. Particularly in the United States, Britain and other Western countries, the cities have undergone many changes during the post war period. Due to increasing industrialisation the heavy inflow of the rural migrants the cities caused slum development. The inner parts were deteriorating at faster rate due to the increasing blight in the neighbourhood. To prevent this urban decay, renewal and redevelopment was attempted on priority basis in large scale by public agencies. The replacement of old and obsolescent housing through redevelopment caused many conflicts and social problems in shifting and relocating the urban poor of the deteriorated parts.

Urban renewal and redevelopment has generated to many ideological conflicts in the developed countries and it has been analysed in its multi-faceted dimension by many people. James Wilson observed it as deep planning process which is embodied in politics. This has been started as good politics but turned into something which at best is difficult politics. He also pointed out that this process subsidizes the high income group and hurts low income group and endangers the right of private property giving rise to certain basic political issues.[8]

Tom Hancock examined the consequences of the replacement of old and obsolescent housing through redevelopment by new public housing in U.K.[9] A policy of housing rehabilitation and selected renewal seemed to offer greater advantage and to be a better alternative to redevelopment when demolition is not absolutely necessary, particularly in view of the heavy cost involved. He also observed that the process of improvement programmes the original occupants have not benefited much but a new comer enjoyed the fruits. Large areas of working class housing, particualry in London, has transformed into newly desirable areas for higher-income households. Therefore, he opines that quiet and gradual change in the city is less destructive of people and communites.

Scott Greer in his study on Urban Renewal and American Cities had surveyed a complex programme of urban renewal spread among hundreds of Amercian Cities.[10] The urban redevelopment and renovation of CBD and implementation problems of renewal programmes have been discussed in detail. He studied the problem in the light of social trends and local communities. He advocates that the urban renewal is a noval effort, we must look at it from several angles as an aspiration, as an organization and as given result. As we shall see, many more side-effects occur in the implementations of the legitimatized aspiration of urban renewal programme and must be seen carefully within the framework of massive social trends. He feels that the redevelopment of our cities depends mostly upon planned public action.

The modern city is sometimes referred to as an *Urban Complex* because the term symbolizes the nature and multiplicity of problems and activities involving the life streams in modern urban societies. Weaver explores the development of cities, analyzes the problems of urban renewal, redevelopment housing and ghetto life and explains the measures to be taken to make the cities more attractive and comfortable for the people who use them. He observes the adverse impact of Urban renewal upon the minorities and low-income group people.[11]

Housing is not a social service. The right to space depends on the ability to pay rather than on need. Jane Darke and Roy Darke investigate all aspects of the housing crisis. They consider the advantages and disadvantages of the major forms of housing tenure.[12] They look at the building industry and criticise the planners, architects, housing agencies for their limited understanding of the real roots of the housing crisis. They opine that while decent housing for all will not be achieved while the capitalist system exists, there is considerable potential for those in housing need to improve their situation through collective action.

The city as a physical entity inherits a catelogue of problems that are among the stable cliches of the society: substandard and deteriorating housing; air and water pollution; urban sprawl, etc. Urban renewal and redevelopment is an almost universal agreement to combat the physical decay of the inner cities. Jewel Bellush and Murray Hausknecht examines the problem in depth in their edited volume on Urban Renewal : People, Politics and Planning. They evaluate the concept in its historical perspective and discuss about its goals and expectations. Execution problems in the context of U.S.A. cities has been viewed in terms of relocation and rehabilitation of the displaced people due to the urban renewal projects.[13]

Coleman Woodbury examined the urban redevelopment of American cities in its early stage with a broader perspective.[14] He identifies redevelopment as those policies, measures and activities that would do away with the major forms of physical blight in cities and bring about changes in urban structure and institutions contributing to a favourable environment for a healthy civic, economic and social life for all urban dwellers. He surveyed the causes of blight and problems of clearance, rehabilitation, relocation, conservation and enforcement of federal programmes. He also suggests that the urban redevelopment is a long-term, continuing process that requires continuous planning.

Slum housing and Residential Renewal: The case in Urban Britain is an important contribution in the field of urban renewal by David A.Kirby.[15] He reviews the historical and socio-economic aspects of sub-standard housing. He examines the nature and role of slum, the process of absolescence, the establishment of minimum fitness standards, the filtering concept and new building, slum clearance and residdential rehabilitation. The case study shows how residential renewal has been tackled in Britain and includes an assessment of the changing size and nature of the slum problem.

Rapid urban redevelopment often has serious adverse effects on the majority of the working population, especially in the poorer countries. William Lim (1975) expresses concern over the large disparity in income distribution and the provision of urban facilities between the privileged elites and the majority of the urban population.[16] He discusses the problem with special reference to ASEAN countries and Singapore.

During recent times some Indian authors have also made detailed and critical studies on the urban renewal and redevelopment with special reference to the Indian metropolitan cities.

Urban renewal, as a concept, has posed a challenge at once, to the art and science of management, planning, architecture and engineering. M.A.Muttalib observes the concept as an ideology, a public policy and a process.[17] The term is used interchangeably with redevelopment and rehabilitations and also with conservation. He denotes that the health of urban settlement can be tested on the basis of quality of civic life and status of urban property. The quality of civic life may decline due to high density of population, inadequacy of community services and their poor maintenance, etc. The decay of urban property becomes visible with the obsolescence of buildings either due to misuse, non-use or disuse. He argues for the acceptance of renewal and redevelopment programmes as a development necessity. He identifies the reasons for the declining and decaying of old city of Hyderabad and evaluates the measures taken by the local authorities in this direction. He proposes the priorities for redevelopment and improving the quality of life. He also recommends the guidelines to be followed by the government and local authorities for economic regeneration, resource mobilisation and managing urban decline in the old city of Hyderabad.

Satish Sinha (1985) observes that the urban renewal includes preservation, rehabilitation of property or environment and redevelopment. The process of renewal and redevelopment gradually changes the character of the area to fit in with the needs of contemporary society. Although the renewal programme involves several types of techniques and projects but the chief emphasis is given to residential redevelopment. He made a comprehensive survey on the problem of urban renewal and slum eradication in Patna city and suggests a short-term and a long-term plan for slum eradication and urban renewal.[18]

Ravindra Prasad (1989) has stressed for the comprehensive redevelopment of physical and social infrastructure of the inner cities. The neglect of central areas of major cities had adverse impact on their physical and socio-economic conditions. He has choosen the selections from the work of numerous authorities to illustrate the conflicting points of view on the problem of urban renewal. These selection examine the philosophy, approaches, and experience of the concept in the Indian context.[19]

The council of Tall buildings (U.S.A. 1981) under the chief editorship of Lynn S.Beedle brought out a significant monographs on high-rise buildings.[20] In addition to the structural design they have also studied the planning and environmental criteria for high-rise buildings. They examine the role of the tall buildings in urban habitat and its interaction with urban systems.

Jaswant B.Mehta (1978) has tried to explain the vital aspects of high-rise buildings with special reference to the Indian social and economic conditions.[21] He feels that for most of the downtown and midtown areas of our large metropolitan cities time has come to demolish the old, existing low-rise, ill-planned buildings constructed around the beginning of this century or the end of the ninteenth century and replace them with well planned, taller multistoreyed buildings capable of rehousing the existing population and allowing enough open space for other uses. He also argues in favour of higher floor area ratio in case of tall buildings as they are intended for creation of more space with optimum land utilization.

Robert C.Williamson (1978) examines the socialization in the high-rise with the emphasis on choice of specific settings, i.e. the preference for given floors, social and community participation, the nature of family relationships and degree of satisfaction or dissatisfaction.[22] He observes that people prefers upper floors mostly with the desire for a view and escape from noise. The high-rise buildings will have limited appeal to those in the child-rearing stage of the life who have strong needs cycle and to those of neighbourliness. He suggests that reduced density and improved design could strengthen tenure.

William S.W.Lim (1975) while observing the relevance of tall buildings in urban growth prefers the low-rise buildings for the developing countries.[23] Tall buildings are more expensive and take longer to construct. Whereas low-rise buildings can be constructed more cheaply using more unskilled and semi-skilled labour. He also argues that the urban centres consisting mainly low-rise buildings tend to have less traffic congestion, less pollution and a more human urban environment.

Daniel Cappon (1972) examines the problem of mental health in the high-rise.[24] For him high-rise apartments certainly appear simpler to define operationally, but its unique no relation with environments create adverse psychological effect. Gerda Wekerle and Edward Hall (1972) examines the high-rise living whether the same design serve young and old.[25] They find the high- satisfaction group generally included young tenants who are single or young married couples on the contrary the low-satisfaction group was composed of older and more stable tenants.

In many inner-city neighbourhoods of North America and Europe, Urban redevelopment most often means that 'dilapidated' housing - mainly walkup apartments or private houses converted to apartments -

is replaced with high-rise elevator apartments. Yet the social consequences of high-rise living as well as data on the satisfaction or dissatisfaction of tenants is virtually unknown.

Objectives and Hypotheses of the study

Indian cities are slowly changing their ageing inner parts with renewed redeveloped sturctures which revitalise the functional force of the city to a required level. The vertical development has become inevitable to meet the growing needs of the city. In Hyderabad city though the redevelopment process of inner city is in infant stage and recent one the overall change is considerble and many huge new multi-storeyed complexes have come up after demolishing the old structures. As such there may be considerable change in the social, economic and commercial values of such areas. The study is aimed to evaluate and identify the social and economic effects due to the redevelopment by way of high-rise buildings. The study specifically aim at the following objectives:

1. To examine the role of high-rise development in the redevelopment process in the city.
2. To examine the social and economic characteristics of the high-rise residents.
3. To examine the structure and trends in commercial space use in high-rise buildings.

The study further will attempt to test the following hypotheses:

1. Urban redevelopment help to boost the commercial value of the land and as a result accessible only to large commercial establishments.
2. High density residential use causes tremendous strains on the infrastructure facilities in the city. It may also cause social and psychological problems to the residents.

Methodology

The High-rise culture in Hyderabad city is a recent one and it took place in the developed areas only. This process has been assumed as a pure consequence of urban redevelopment. This process has been examined in three defferent angles. First as a process of vertical development in which the problems are analysed developers point of view. The second and third aspects are the high-rise development for commercial use and the living in high-rise buildings respectively have been attempted on the basis of social and spatial form.

Investigations included desk studies, interviews with key professionals and residents and their representatives, questionnaire survey and systematic site observations. The survey with questionnaires included three categories, one with residents of high-rise buildings, second on commercial units in high-rise buildings and the other related to the developers. The main intension of the study was to obtain the residents views on high-rise living and to observe difficuties faced by them in the first case. Many people who are involved in this new trend of high-rise development have been interviewed personally, in order to ascertain their views regarding the social, economic and wider environmental impacts of the high-rise complexes which reflect redevelopment.

The bricks and mortar of the current study are almost entirely supplied by the respondents to the questionnaires. The questionnaires used in the survey was structured with a view to obtain information necessary to achieve the objectives of the study. The study is also based on data collected from a large number of government and other organisational sources. The second sources of information from which the required data collected includes Census of India, Municipal Corporation of Hyderabad, Quli Qutub Shah Urban Development Authority, Hyderabad Urban Development Authority, Town Planning Department and Andhra Pradesh Housing Board, etc. The area within Municipal limits has been taken as study area and the problems/phenomena are examind taking the ward as a unit of study. A trifurcation of the city into three distinct zones, Hyderabad South, Hyderabad North and Secunderabad which reveal three different characteristics has been made for highlighting the spatial differentiation in the present study.

Primary survey by means of questionnaires has been conducted on sample basis. Since most of the high-rise units concentrated in the city centre and its adjacent wards, the survey covered almost all the units by selecting about 10 percent households in each unit. The survey of commercial units and developers is also made on random sample basis. The simplest type of probability sampling, where the probabilities associated with different possible samples are equal is called random sampling.

Statistical data on the high-rise buildings used in the study has been collected through personal visit to all parts of the city. The information such as the use, number of floors and the age of building, etc. is collected personally by covering the total areas of the city as the recorded data on all aspects was not available.

The data collected from both primary and secondary sources has been processed and in the analysis suitable statistical and cartographic techniques have been employed. Different socio-economic variables have been used as indicators to derive the standard of living, level of satisfaction, physical and social disadvantages etc. in assessing the housing and neighbourhood conditions. The data has also been represented by maps and diagrams, wherever necessary using cartographic techniques for symbolic representation.

REFERENCES

1. Donald H.Webster, *Urban Planning and Municipal Public Policy*, Harper & Bros. Publishers, New York, 1958.
2. Coleman Woodbury, *Urban Redevelopment: Problems and Practices*, The University of Chicago Press, Chicago, 1962.
3. Ibid.
4. Tom Hamcock (Ed.), *Growth and change in the future city Region*, London, Leonard Hill, 1976.
5. Scott Greer, *Urban Renewal and American cities*, The Bobbs- Merrill Co. Inc., New York, 1980.
6. Ibid.
7. Stuart chapin, F. Jr., *Urban Landuse Planning*, Harper and Bors., New York, 1957.
8. James Q. Wilson, The Reocrd and the Controversy, The MIT Press, Massachusetts Institute of Technology, Cambridge, Massachusetts, 1964.
9. Ibid.
10. Ibid.
11. Robert C. Weaver, The Urban Complex, Doubleday & Company Inc., New York, 1964.
12. Jane Darke and Roy Darke, *Who needs housing?*, The Macmillan Press Limited, London, *1979*.
13. Jewel Bellush & Murray Hausknecht, *Urban Renewal: People, Politics and Planning*', Doubleday and Co. Inc., New York, 1967.
14. *Ibid.*
15. David A.Kirby, *Slum Housing and Residential: The Case in Urban Britain*, Longman group Ltd., London, 1979.
16. William S.W. Lim, 'Tall Buildings for Urban centres in Third World countries', *Ekistics*, Vol. No. 40, No. 238, 1975, pp. 196-198.
17. Muttalib, M.A., *Urban Renewal: A Case Study for the old city of Hyderabad*, Regional Centre for Urban & Environmental Studies, Hyderabad.
18. Satish, Sinha, *Slum Eradication and Urban Renewal: Patna*, Inter-India Publications, New Delhi.
19. Ravindra Prasad, D. (Ed.), *Urban Renewal: The Indian Experience*, Sterling Publishers Pvt. Ltd., New Delhi, 1989.
20. Lynn S. Beedle, (Ed.), Planning & Environmental criteria for Tall Buildings, Vol. PC of Monograph on Planning and Design of Tall Buildings, ASCE, New York, 1981.
21. Jaswant B. Mehta, *High-rise Buildings*, Skyline, Bombay, 1978.
22. Robert C. Williamson, 'Socialization in the high-rise: A cross-national comparison', *Ekistics*, Vol. 45, No. 268, 1978, pp. 122-130.
23. *Ibid.*
24. Daniel Cappon, Mental Health in the High-rise, *Ekistics*, No. 196, 1972, pp. 192-195.
25. Gerda Wekerle & Edward Hall, 'High-rise Living: Can the Same Design Serve Young & Old; *Ekistics*, No. 196, 1972.

2

GEOGRAPHICAL BACKGROUND

Location and Physical Environment

Hyderabad, the capital of Andhra Pradesh State of India, occupies a unique position and is one of the leading metropolitan cities of India. It is, being the primate city of Andhra Pradesh, one of the strategically located industrial centres in South India.

Hyderabad is situated in the heart of the Deccan Plateau at an average height of 540 (1760 feet) metres above mean sea level. The city is located at 17°20′N latitude and 78°30′E longitude, covering an area of 217 sq.kms. approximately. (Fg.2.1)

The twin cities Hyderabad-Secunderabad stand on pink and grey granites, which is suitable for constructions. The granitic hills are spread all over the city and its surrounding areas. The River Musi is a tributory of River Krishna, passes through the heart of the city thereby bisecting it into two significant parts. Hyderabad is a city of glittering lakes. Among these Osmansagar and Himayatsagar, which are fresh water tanks, are the chief source of drinking water. These reserviors were constructed after the devastating flood in the Musi in 1908. These reserviors, located at a distance of about 16 kms. west of Hyderabad are now not only the sources of water supply to the twin cities but are also used by the public as picnic resort. The flow of River Musi from west to east attests to the general slope of the city which is eastward.

The city has a generally warm and dry climate. The daily maximum temperature varies from a minimum of 12°C during the month of December to a maximum of 43°C during the month of May. The average humidity round the year varies between a maximum of 75 per cent and a minimum of 47 per cent. The daily maximum humidity in the morning varies from 53 per cent in April to 83 per cent during July-September. The months of April to October during which period the temperature is rather high gets rain from south-west monsoon. The city receives about 770mm. of rainfall in a normal year.

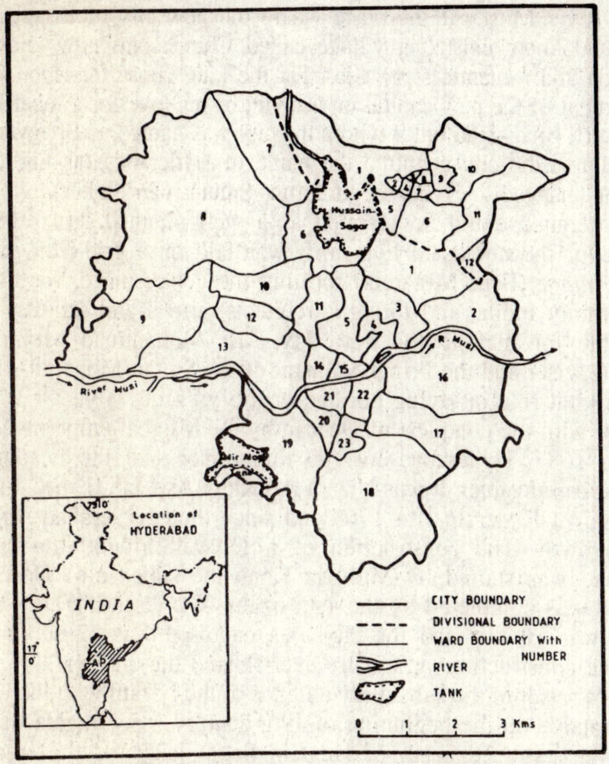

Fig. 2.1 : Hyderabad City—Location Map

Historical Background

Hyderabad city, with a history of four centuries has experienced many political, economic and socio-culturual upheavals. Hyderabad city as is known at present did not exist 400 years ago. The area must have been largely covered by undulating rocky gorund with jungle growth and some old villages located here and there around which were some green fields and archards. It was one of the local Governors of the Bahamani Rulers, Sultan Quli Qutub Shah who established his headquarters at Golconda with the breaking up of Bahamani rule, Sultan Quli Qutub Shah established his own independent kingdom of Golconda in 1518, and improved the Golconda Fort.

As the Fort became conjested, on a representation by the Nobles, it is believed that the V ruler of Golconda, Mohammad Quli Qutub Shah, founded the city of Bhagyanagar in A.D. 1591 on the southern

Bank of River Musi. At the place where the new city of Bhagyanagar was located, there existed a village called Chinchalam now known as Shalibanda and romantic story goes that the king chose this spot for the establishment of the new capital on account of his love for a local Hindu dancing girl, Bhagamati, after whom the city was named as Bhagyanagar. In due course the city acquired the name of Hyderabad (as his lover's name was changed to Hyder Begum after Sultan married her).

Hyderabad could be claimed as a well planned city primarily intended for the nobles to live in. It was laid on a grid-iron pattern, the *Charminar* (Four Minarets) forming the centre-piece, for its four portals. Many Indian and foreign architects, artists and scholars were responsible for making the new city. Mir Mohammad Momin the spiritual adviser and the Prime Minister of the Sultan Mohammad Quli played a vital role in laying out and beautifying the city.

But with the conquest of Deccan by the Moghal emperor Aurangazeb in 1687, Hyderabad lost its importance and the headquarter shifted to Aurangabad. It was Nizam Ali Khan Asif Jah II who restored the capital of Hyderabad in 1763 and since then Hyderabad shown a steady growth. The construction of a fortwall around the city of Hyderabad was started by Mubariz Khan the subedar of Deccan in 1712 and was completed by the 1st Nizam. The circumference of the fortwall was 10 km. and the city area enclosed was 12 sq.km. The residential constructions gradually over-flowed the city wall.

As a result of the subsidiary alliance of the Nizam with the British paramountancy in the beginning of 19th century a contingent of 5000 troops was stationed north of Hussain Sagar lake and the area was named as Secunderabad after the name of the Nizam Sikandar Jah. Simultaneously with the creation of Secunderabad, the British residency was constructed on the northern banks of river Musi which helped residential and commercial development in the adjacent areas. The opening up of railway and location of terminal stations at Nampally and Kachiguda for the broad guage and metre guage rail lines saw further extension of the city in those directions.

Hyderabad city had the previlege of the reservoirs, city improvement schemes, as well as the drainage scheme masterminded by the late Sri Mokshagundam Visveshwarayya, the eminent engineer and economist and his colleague Nawab Ali Nawaz Jung who was the chief engineer of great repute. A major political upheaval in the history of Hyderabad is the police Action in 1948. This ended the era of the Nizam's rule and the Hyderabad State was integrated with rest of the Indian Union. With the adoption as capital of Andhra Pradesh state, Hyderabad city has grown into a leading metropolitan centre by restoring its position of primacy.

The city developed into a multi-nucleated urban centre of the region under different political, economic and socio-cultural conditions which added new ingredients into its modern urban complex. The people of Hyderabad are an epitome of the diverse cultures of India. We find the real confluence of northern and southern cultures of India in this city. The twin cities of Hyderabad and Secunerabad each have had different historical backgrounds. Hyderabad with a medieval origin grew mostly under Muslim feudal rule, while Secunderabad developed mainly under British influence. The growth of the twin cities of Hyderabad and Secunderabad has thus been influenced by differing historical, social and economic factors.

Spatial Growth and Evolution of City

Hyderabad city right from its inception in 1591 by Mohammad Quli Qutub Shah, was in continuous growth except for the period 1687 to 1724 which was known as the dark ages of city. (Fg.2.2) The city was planned on grid pattern, with Charminar in the centre. All kinds of amenities that were necessary for a good living were provided. Its prosperity and development must have come to an end with the decline of the Qutub Shahi kingdom concurrent with the Moghul invasion towards the middle of 17th century.

After shifting the capital of State from Aurangabad to Hyderabad during the period of Nizam Ali Khan Asaf Jah, the city regained its momentum and experienced continuous growth since then.

Hyderabad city developed in two phases of twin settlements. The first was the Golconda-Hyderabad phase covering the period A.D. 1591 to A.D. 1687 and the second was the Hyderabad-Secunderabad phase comprising the period A.D. 1798 to A.D. 1940. The first phase saw Hyderabad over shadowing Golconda, reducing the later to a dormitory suburb in ruins. The second phase witnessed the incessant political and economic interaction between two distinctive cultures, native and alien. The full way of integrating forces culminated in the political fusion of Hyderabad and Secunderabad through an Act of the Local Legislature in 1960.

Though the initial growth was east-west along the commercial highway to Masulipatnam, with the formation of Secunderabad and construction of bridges on the Musi river, the shift in the growth towards North-South was distinct and a continuous process. The destruction caused by floods in 1908 has a beneficial impact on the future growth and development of the city. Consequently for the planned development of the city the City Improvement Board was constituted in the year 1912, which had taken steps to remove the slums and other residential

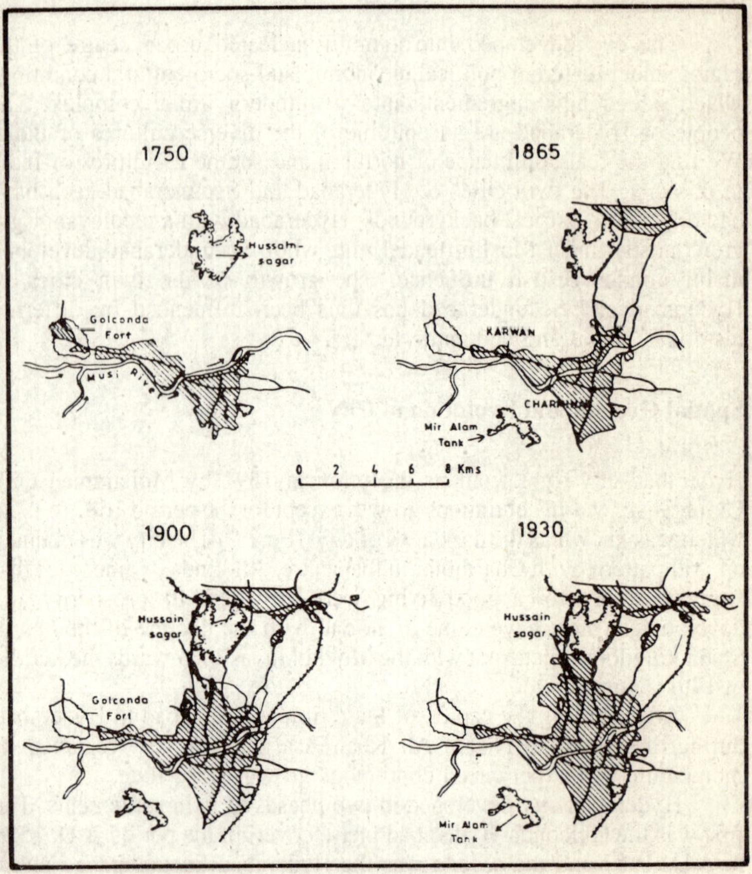

Fig. 2.2 : Hyderabad City—Spatial Growth

areas, most vulnerable to floods and provide them shelter in planned residential colonies. The areas along the river bank were converted into parks and play grounds.

In the vicinity of British residency a good residential area came up later which became the focal point for the development of new elite residential district as there was a large migration of nobles and top officials to this area from the old city.

Hyderabad experienced a tremendous growth after the formation of Andhra Pradesh in 1956. After independence Hyderabad has emerged not only as an administrative centre but it has developed into a major industrial centre also. Many private and public sector industrial units are located here. With this the city attracted many people and it caused a large influx of migration. The number of suburban settlements or agglomeration units have increased as a consequence of tremendous population growth. It resulted in not only peripheral growth, but there has been an intensification of residential and commercial activities in the city core also.

At present Hyderabad city consists of 35 municipal wards including 12 wards of Secunderabad covering an area of 169.16 sq.kms.

Hyderabad town group now comprises the integrated Municipal Corporation of Hyderabad with 3.1 million population and eleven other neighbouring urban settlements making up an area of 252 sq.kms. and a total population of 4.2 million according to 1991 census. More spatial changes and also changes in the skyline of the city have taken place during the last two decades. Particularly the central parts of the city have undergone drastic changes as the vertical development is a distinctive phenomena during the last decade. A large number of multi-storeyed residential apartments and commercial complexes have sprung up in and around the central city. Mainly, this is due to the intensification of commercial and residential use in the most developed areas of the city. Space requirement to meet the residential and commercial demands has stimulated the vertical expansion.

The present skyline of Hyderabad city specially around central areas is full of multi-storeyed buildings of various functions. The new development taking place today is mostly away from the historic core. The southern part of the city is relatively a static region.

Growth of Population

The spatial growth of the city is directly related to its population growth. Hyderabad being a centrally located city of India, has been continuously receiving a number of migrants from all over India right from its inception. But the inordinate growth in population of the city is seen after the formation of Andhra Pradesh State. The figures given in Table 2.1 (Fig. 2.3) shows the growth for a period of one century. However, there is steady positive growth throughout this period, except during one decade 1911-21, when the city registered a decline of 19.21 per cent in population. This may be due to major epidemics—plague and cholera occurred in the early part of the period and influenza in 1918-19. There upon a steady growth is recorded. Though there was 15.10 per cent increase in population during 1921-31 decade, the population remained below the 1911 level. The epidemic trouble was not checked during this peirod also. The next two decades witnessed over 50 per cent bulge each in the city population. Subsequently the growth of population was steady once again. Consequent on the states reorganisation in 1956 the pace of growth of Hyderabad both in population and area has been accelerated. The acceleration in the growth rate of city in recent past can be linked up with the process of rapid industrialization and its administrative functions.

TABLE 2.1 : Growth of Population in Hyderabad, 1881-1991

Year	Population	Percent decade variation
1881	3,67,417	—
1891	4,15,039	12.65
1901	4,48,466	3.29
1911	5,02,104	11.96
1921	4,05,630	–19.21
1931	4,66,894	15.10
1941	7,20,032	60.94
1951	10,26,062	42.50
1961	11,18,553	9.01
1971	16,12,276	44.14
1981	21,50,058	33.81
1991	30,91,718	37.35

Source:

1. Census of India, 1931, Hyderabad State, Part-I Report
2. Census of India, 1981, Andhra Pradesh, Part-II General Population Tables
3. Census of India, 1991 Provisional Population Tables

Migration and Population Growth

The growth of population is the result of natural growth and immigration. The city experienced a tremendous influx of migrants after the integration of Hyderabad state with the rest of India and formation of Andhra Pradesh State. Since the city was made capital of the newly formed State of Andhra Pradesh a number of people from other regions have migrated to the city. The large increase in the population during 1941-61 was mainly due to the above reasons. Table 2.2 illustrates the stream of migrants during 1971-81. The proportion of migrants was high in the decade 1961-71, compared to the later period. But the magnitude of migrants at the latter point of time is also considerable.

TABLE 2.2 : Hyderabad City: Migrant Population, 1971-81

	1971	1981
Total Population	16,12,276	21,50,058
No. of migrants	4,09,980	5,07,262
Percent of migrants to total population	22.82	19.93
Percent increase in migrants	31.28	23.73

Source: : Census of India, Andhra Pradesh, Part-XIIi A and B, Village and Town Directory, Hyderabad District, 1981

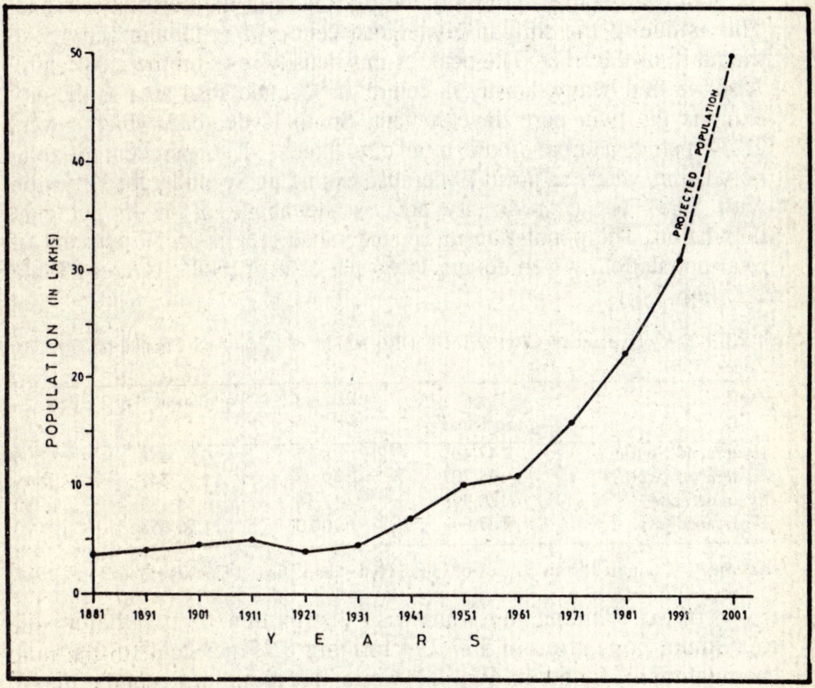

Fig. 2.3 : Hyderabad City—Growth of Population

Demographic Structure and Trends

Population Density and Variation

The total population of Hyderabad city (Municipal Corporation) as of 1981 is 2,150,058 of which 1,814,925 forming 84.41 per cent pertains to Hyderabad division and 3,35,133 forming 15.59 per cent to Secunderabad division. This has gone up to 3,091,718 according to 1991 census.

Hyderabad urban population is 1/4 of the total urban population of the State. Hyderabad city is celebrating the 400th year of its existence with the agglomeration crossing 4 million mark. With the growth during the decade 1981-91 Hyderabad has overtaken Bangalore and Ahmedabad and recaptured its position as the 5th largest city in the Country.

Hyderabad's average density of population is 14,248 per/km^2 in 1991. This has been increased from around 9600 in 1971 to about 11,000 in 1981. Although once the density of population was more in the south Hyderabad, presently we find more in the north Hyderabad. This is due to the shift in Hyderabad centre of economic activity to the north of the river. The peak of this density rests on the city centre. Also we find heavy density in centre of Secunderabad area as the city exhibits the twin core development. South Hyderabad which covers 28.37 per cent area of the total city, holds 31.96 per cent of total population, where as north Hyderabad excluding Secunderabad division with 59.07 per cent of city area is the abode of 52.45 per cent population. The population in Secunderabad area is 15.59 per cent of total population, which covers 12.56 per cent of total city area (Table 2.3, Fig. 2.4).

TABLE 2.3: Hyderabad City: Percent Distribution of Area And Population By City Zones, 1981

Zone	Area (Sq.Kms)	Percent	Population	Percent
Hyderabad South	47.40	28.37	6,87,078	31.96
Hyderabad North	98.70	59.07	11,27,847	52.45
Secunderabad	20.99	12.56	3,35,133	15.59
Hyderabad city	167.09	100.0	21,50,058	100.00

Source: Compiled from Census of India, Hyderabad District Census Hand Book, 1981

If we examine the ward-wise distribution of population the maximum population of 177,299 forming 8.25 per cent to the total population is found in Ward-1 while the minimum population of 7,686 forming 0.36 per cent is found in Ward-3 of Secunderabad division.

As can be seen from Table 2.4 (Fig.2.5), gross densities in Hyderabad city range from as low as 2, 735 persons/km^2 in Ward-8 of Hyderabad division to as high as 60,784 persons/km^2 in the inner wards (No.4) of Secunderabad division as per 1981 census. It is observed that the highest densities occur in the oldest parts of the city. On either side of the Musi river the wards 20, 21, 22, 23, 14 and 15 which form the oldest parts of the Hyderabad division registers the population density of above 40,000 persons/km.^{2} The older parts of the Secunderabad also exhibits the same trend. However, the core areas of the city in the northern zone show higher densities with gradual

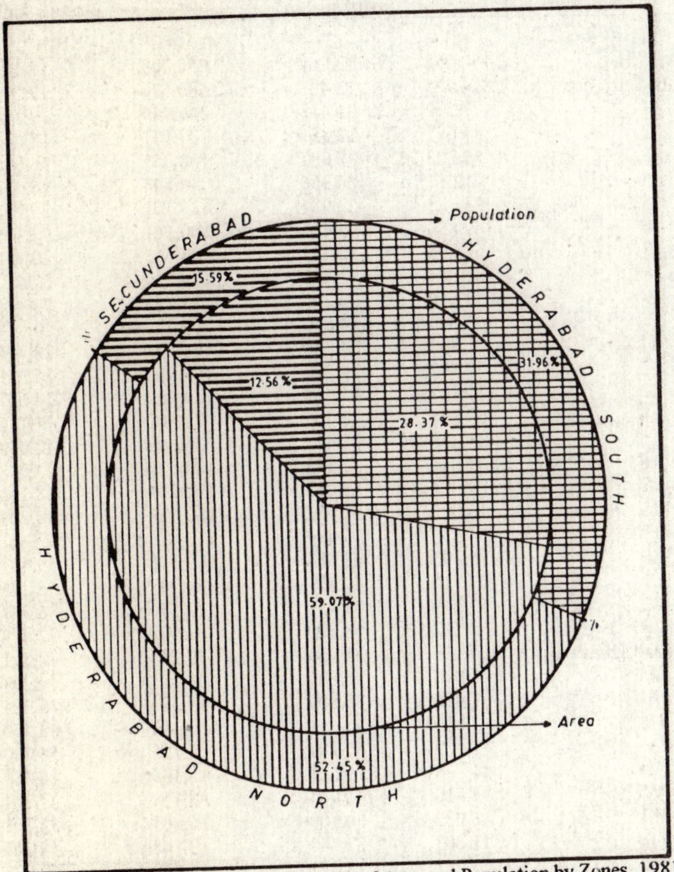

Fig. 2.4 : Hyderabad City—Distribution of Area and Population by Zones, 1981

decrease towards peripheral areas. On the whole 26 wards out of 35 wards in Hyderabad Corporation have higher density than the city in average, other 9 wards have lower density. The estimated figures for ward-wise population and density for 1991 (Fig.2.6) are given in the same table. A considerable increase in the density for inner wards of Hyderabad South and North zones is noticed.

TABLE 2.4 : Hyderabad City: Density of Population by City Wards, 1981 and 1991

City Ward No.	1981		1991 (Estimated)	
	Population	Density persons km^2	Population	Density persons km^2
(1)	(2)	(3)	(4)	(5)
M.C.H.	2,150,058	12,867	3,059,783	18,105
Hyderabad division	1,814,925	12,422	2,580,529	17,554
1	177,299	21,412	245,949	29,704
2	87,677	12,855	127,131	18,640
3	89,203	32,087	100,353	36,098
4	41,911	24,366	44,844	26,072
5	73,781	22,984	83,151	25,903
6	69,806	6,439	100,171	9,240
7	52,905	12,389	88,615	20,752
8	82,784	2,735	198,599	6,563
9	54,850	4,790	85,785	7,492
10	63,646	14,870	89,231	20,848
11	57,490	24,780	66,803	28,794
12	57,492	19,100	107,912	35,851
13	110,897	15,663	174,219	24,607
14	69,848	46,565	77,601	51,734
15	38,258	43,475	36,995	42,039
16	134,644	17,195	187,828	23,988
17	129,067	19,092	190,244	28,142
18	110,002	6,922	162,143	10,204
19	64,338	5,489	112,076	9,562
20	75,793	48,585	92,770	59,467
21	49,317	49,815	54,742	55,295
22	59,215	38,451	72,360	46,987
23	64,702	58,290	81,007	72,979
Secunderabad Division	335,133	15,966	479,254	22,821
I	38,073	5,509	54,101	7,829
II	11,456	35,800	11,304	35,325
III	7,686	45,211	7,390	43,470
IV	7,902	60,784	7,115	54,730
V	11,738	11,621	15,130	14,980
VI	44,910	21,084	58,158	27,304
VII	16,032	50,100	16,865	52,703
VIII	11,603	52,740	12,148	55,218
IX	13,917	18,311	14,877	19,575
X	36,530	10,904	47,489	14,175
XI	44,795	34,996	86,544	67,612
XII	90,491	20,612	148,133	33,743

Source: Census of India, Hyderabad DCH, 1981

Table 2.5 or Fig. 2.7 shows ward-wise population variation during 1971-81. The percent population increase was relatively higher in the peripheral wards compared to the core city wards both in Hyderabad and Secunderabad. The central core wards registered less population increase because of the rapid encroachment of commercial landuse

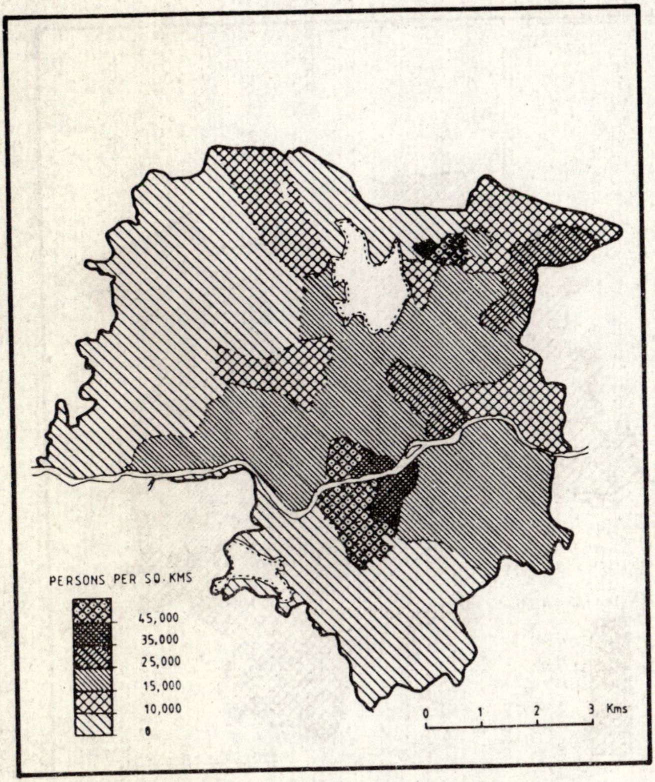

Fig. 2.5 : Hyderabad City : Density of Population, 1981

along the main thoroughfare and their adjoining areas. In Secunderabad ward Nos 2, 3 and 4 have registered population less due to large scale displacement of residential areas by the expanding commercial complexes, thereby shifting residential use to peripheral areas. On the contrary the peripheral wards have registered a phenomenal increase in population. Three contiguous wards 7, 8 and 9 in Hyderabad North have registered enormous increase in population. This may be due to the close proximity to industrial areas such as Kukatpally, Santhnagar, etc. and Government offices.

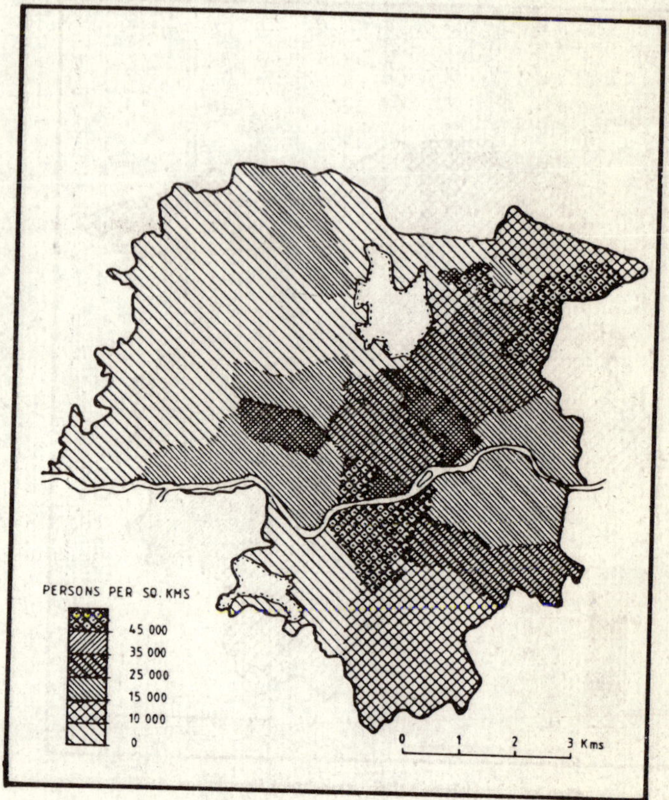

Fig. 2.6 : Hyderabad City : Density of Population, 1991

Sex Composition

According to 1981 census, Hyderabad Corporation area has a general sex composition of 920 females to 1000 males. This has been slightly decreased as per 1991 census as we find 918 females to 1000 males. A careful examination of ward-wise distribution of sex composition as noted in Table 2.6 (Fig. 2.8) shows that it ranges from 901 to 1041 females to 1000 males. Secunderabad, South Hyderabad and also central part of the city is having higher sex-ratio values as compared to the other areas. Industrial areas are showing the lesser values as the more male working population concentrates in these areas. It is also observed that in all wards except ward-9 in Secunderabad division males out number the females.

TABLE 2.5 : Hyderabad City: Population Variation, 1971-81

Ward No.	Population		Percent variation 1971-81
	1981	1971	
Hyderabad Division	1,814,925	1,356,760	33.77
1	1,77,299	131,219	35.12
2	87,677	62,004	41.41
3	89,203	81,918	8.89
4	41,911	40,526	3.42
5	73,781	67,633	9.09
6	69,806	49,920	39.84
7	52,905	32,283	63.88
8	82,784	35,037	136.28
9	54,850	35,895	52.81
10	63,646	46,649	36.64
11	57,490	51,075	12.56
12	57,492	31,227	84.11
13	110,897	72,228	53.54
14	69,848	64,977	7.50
15	38,258	39,574	(-) 3.33
16	134,644	99,055	35.93
17	129,067	88,442	45.93
18	110,002	76,476	43.84
19	64,338	37,714	70.59
20	75,793	63,823	18.75
21	49,317	45,939	7.35
22	59,215	49,918	18.62
23	64,702	53,228	21.56
Secunderabad Division	335,133	250,636	33.71
I	38,073	27,486	38.52
II	11,456	11,611	(-) 1.33
III	7,686	7,994	(-) 3.85
IV	7,902	8,776	(-) 9.96
V	11,738	9,368	25.30
VI	44,910	35,658	25.95
VII	16,032	15,775	1.63
VIII	11,603	11,473	1.13
IX	13,917	13,475	3.28
X	36,530	28,892	26.44
XI	44,795	23,619	89.66
XII	90,491	56,509	60.14

Source : Census of India, A.P., Hyderabad District Census Hand Book, 1981

Literacy

The percentage of literates in the city in 1981 calculated on the total population of all ages works out to 57.79 per cent which is 5 per cent more

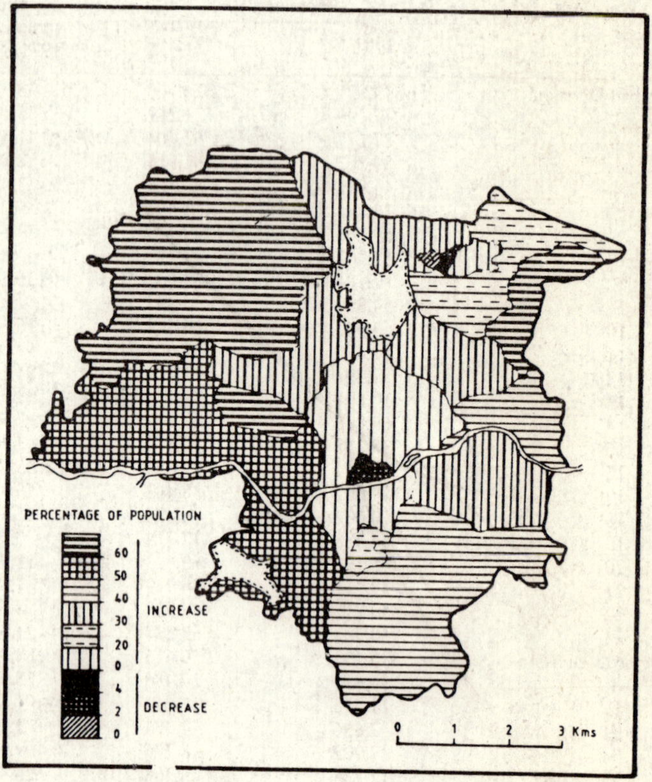

Fig. 2.7 : Hyderabad City : Population Variation, 1971-81

than that recorded in the previous decade. Secunderabad division has recorded a higher rate of literacy with 62.09 per cent while in Hyderabad division it is 57 per cent (Table 2.7, Fig. 2.9). The literacy rate among males is 66.03 per cent while among females it is 48.95 per cent. According to 1991 census the total literacy percentage of the city population is 55.03 per cent among which males percentage is 61.88 and females percentage is 47.58. The slight decrease in the literacy level may be due to the inflow of illiterate rural migrants.

TABLE 2.6: Hyderabad City: Ward-wise Sex Ratio, 1981

Ward No.	Males	Females	Sex Ratio (Females per 1000 males)
Hyderabad Division	942,349	872,576	926
1	91,692	85,607	934
2	45,507	42,170	927
3	45,992	43,211	940
4	21,750	20,161	927
5	38,477	35,304	918
6	36,125	33,681	932
7	27,775	25,130	905
8	42,763	40,021	936
9	33,901	20,949	618
10	32,600	31,046	952
11	29,532	27,958	947
12	29,686	27,803	936
13	57,139	53,758	941
14	36,112	33,736	934
15	19,830	18,428	929
16	69,415	65,229	940
17	66,328	62,739	946
18	56,714	53,288	940
19	33,393	30,945	927
20	38,612	37,181	963
21	25,297	24,020	950
22	30,453	28,762	944
23	33,253	31,449	946
Secunderabad Division	171,295	163,838	956
I	19,796	18,277	923
II	5,825	5,631	967
III	3,962	3,724	940
IV	4,045	3,857	954
V	6,011	5,727	953
VI	22,988	21,922	954
VII	8,434	7,598	901
VIII	5,901	5,702	966
IX	6,818	7,099	1,041
X	18,336	18,194	992
XI	22,828	21,967	962
XII	46,351	44,140	952

Source: Census of India, A.P., Hyderabad District Census Hand Book, 1981

Density of Residential Houses

The average density of residential houses in Hyderabad city is 8.27 per acre as per 1981 census. This was found to be 5.72 in 1971. Table 2.8 (Fig. 2.10) denotes that the higher densities are found in the oldest residential areas. In Hyderabad division they are found around the Charminar, and in Secunderabad division, the highest residential densities are found in

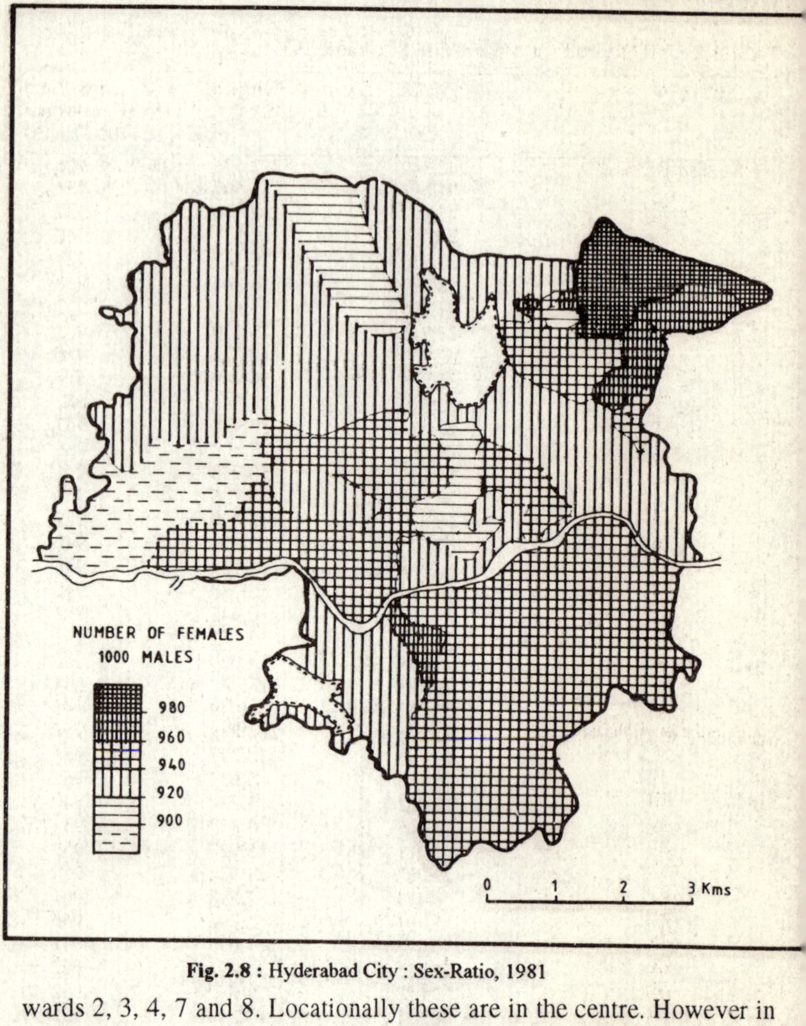

Fig. 2.8 : Hyderabad City : Sex-Ratio, 1981

wards 2, 3, 4, 7 and 8. Locationally these are in the centre. However in the central parts of the Secunderabad division considerable decrease is noted in the residential density compared to 1971 figures. This may be due to the conversion of older residential units into the large commercial complexes. On the contrary, we find a steady increase in all the wards in Hyderabad division. While the central parts register higher densities, gradual decrease is noticed towards peripheral areas. An accute over-crowding of residential dwellings is noticed in the wards, 3, 4, 5, 14 and 15 in Northern zone and 20, 21, 22 and 23 of Southern zone of Hyderabad. A density of 15 houses per acre has been recommended as a maximum by the State Housing Board. In Secunderabad high density is found in many

TABLE 2.7 : Hyderabad City: Ward-wise Distribution of Literates, 1981

Ward No.	Population	Percent of Literates Males	Females	Total
Hyderabad Division	1,814,925	65.24	48.10	57.00
1	177,299	69.54	51.91	61.03
2	87,677	69.17	52.62	61.23
3	89,203	75.25	61.35	68.52
4	41,911	77.49	62.95	70.49
5	73,781	63.67	49.82	57.04
6	69,806	67.07	50.54	59.10
7	52,905	72.91	56.61	65.16
8	82,784	59.27	41.19	50.53
9	54,850	75.09	42.99	62.83
10	63,646	70.13	56.48	63.42
11	57,490	66.76	52.00	59.58
12	57,492	64.12	48.30	56.47
13	110,897	52.73	32.08	42.72
14	69,848	58.33	36.95	48.00
15	38,258	73.57	49.77	62.10
16	134,644	68.49	54.71	61.82
17	129,067	61.95	45.97	54.18
18	110,002	54.55	33.97	44.58
19	64,338	51.88	35.67	44.09
20	75,793	63.95	47.85	56.05
21	49,317	70.33	52.70	61.74
22	59,215	63.61	50.73	57.35
23	64,702	66.61	52.34	59.68
Secunderabad Division	335,133	70.37	53.44	62.09
I	38,073	72.02	55.11	63.90
II	11,456	68.17	51.16	59.81
III	7,686	74.38	61.17	67.98
IV	7,902	76.66	54.14	65.67
V	11,738	65.50	51.86	58.84
VI	44,910	64.42	49.12	56.95
VII	16,032	69.93	54.40	62.57
VIII	11,603	79.14	62.59	71.01
IX	13,917	79.64	64.59	71.96
X	36,530	63.54	50.37	56.98
XI	44,795	69.63	50.76	60.38
XII	90,491	73.29	54.15	63.95

Source: Census of India, A.P., Hyderabad District Census Hand Book, 1981

places where it ranges between four to forty houses per acre, and seven out of twelve wards exceed the standard residential density recommended by the Andhra Pradesh Housing Board (A.P.H.B). In Hyderabad the residential density varies between two to twenty nine and ten out of twenty three are exceeding the standard residential density.

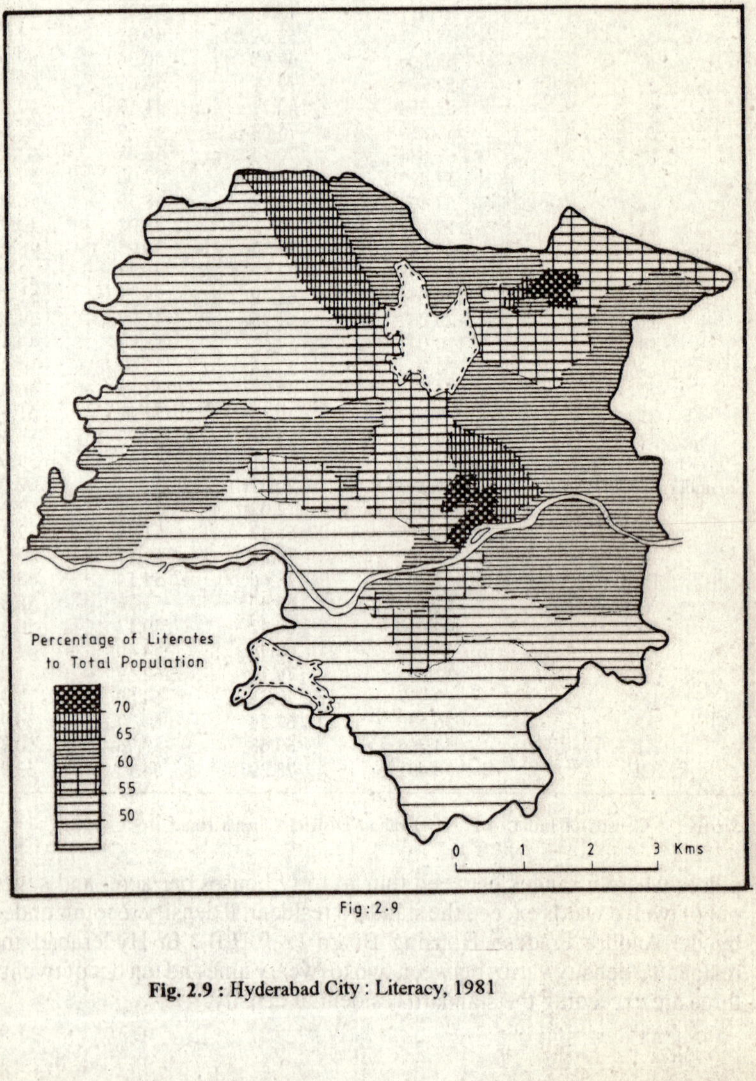

Fig. 2.9 : Hyderabad City : Literacy, 1981

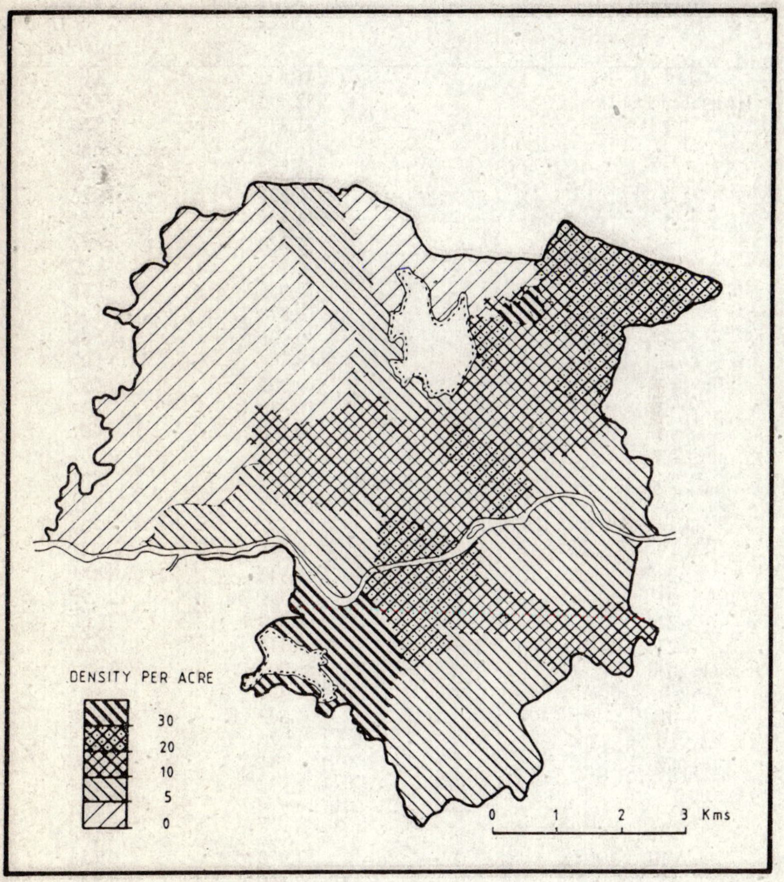

Fig. 2.10 : Hyderabad City : Density of Residential Houses, 1981

TABLE 2.8 : Hyderabad City: Density of Residential Houses, 1981

Ward No.	No. of Residential Houses	Density (No. of Houses per Acre)
M. C. H.	341,499	8.27
Hyderabad Division	282,490	7.92
1	31,837	15.56
2	16,004	9.50
3	15,526	22.55
4	6,901	16.26
5	11,448	15.61
6	11,350	7.22
7	8,755	8.29
8	14,085	1.88
9	6,828	2.38
10	9,605	12.88
11	8,564	14.97
12	9,309	12.50
13	16,348	9.34
14	10,396	28.02
15	6,104	27.91
16	17,443	9.01
17	18,909	11.32
18	17,332	6.09
19	9,501	3.81
20	10,843	27.81
21	7,099	28.98
22	8,659	22.66
23	9,644	28.36
Secunderabad Division	59,009	11.37
I	6,612	3.87
II	1,603	20.29
III	1,076	25.55
IV	1,231	39.70
V	1,878	7.65
VI	7,715	14.64
VII	2,662	33.48
VIII	1,970	35.56
IX	2,160	11.47
X	7,168	8.65
XI	7,880	24.93
XII	17,054	15.72

Source: Census of India. A.P., Hyderabad District Census Hand Book. 1981 (Compiled)

REFERENCES

1. Alam, S.M., *Hyderabad-Secunderabad: A study in Urban Geography*, Allied Publishers Private Limited. 1965.

2. Census of India, Series-2, Andhra Pradesh, Part-XIII A and B, Village and Town Directory, Village and Town Primary Census Abstract, Hyderabad District, 1981, Hyderabad.
3. Development Plan for Hyderabad city, Director of Town Planning, Government of Andhra Pradesh, 1965.
4. Gopi, K.N., *Process of Urban Fringe Development,* Concept Publications, New Delhi, 1978.
5. Gopi, K.N. and Kalpana, M., *Energy, Environment and Human Well-being: An Urban Persepective,* Concept Publishing House, New Delhi.
6. Vijaya Bhole, *Housing and Urban Development in India,* Classical Publishing Company, New Delhi, 1988.
7. Viswanadham, G., *Urban Demography and Ecology: A case study of an Indian city* (Hyderabad), Light and Life Publishers, New Delhi, 1979.

3

REDEVELOPMENT PROCESS AND TRENDS

High-rise Buildings - A process of Redevelopment

During the past few decades almost all the metropolitan cities of India have continued to grow rapidly and are facing formidable problems of lack of basic urban amenities like housing, water supply, etc. caused by increase in population. Hyderabad is also experiencing rapid increase in population and due to this, the city is growing spatially at an alarming pace both vertically and horizontally. Pressure is mounting up because of the land resource in the inner city is getting used up. Therefore, there is an increasing demand on urban land and the absence of adquate land for various uses have resulted in high-rise development.

Redevelopment is one way of treatment of urban decay and restoration of good urban health. Removal of diseased parts is essential for a healthy tissue growth. The response to demand for additional space for shops, offices and residential purpose in the city's central parts has been usually new buildings of greatly increased capacity, i.e. the modern high-rise structures. The central area redevelopment is subject to planning controls and regulations. As land availability becomes less, its cost goes high in the developed parts. Consequently taller constructions are preferred to create more space and to lessen the cost of land component of built area. However, the construction cost may increase as building heights rise. The most economical built forms arise in keeping view the demand, land price and construction cost.

High-rise buildings and their location in the city have been largely unplanned, the product generally of land development pressures. Because of their placement, site planning, development and design have not necessarily been in harmony with the general city plan. They have on some occasions created more problems than they have solved.

The development of the modern city is measured with its vertical growth. Earlier the spiritual and religious structures reached the sky with minarets and spires, but they are no longer the focal point in comtemporary cities. The new focal points are structures which are shaped by industrial and economic priorities. The population pressure in urban areas is the chief cause of this shift.

Initially city grows horizontally. Once it reaches a level of saturation in terms of transportation cost to the central areas and fails in maintaining civic amenities in the peripheral areas, the growth in the central areas starts in vertical direction. The deteriorated and out dated old constructions in these areas tend to be replaced themselves by taller buildings which suits the growing needs. Development of these buildings in Indian cities is very much part of the process of redevelopment.

High-rise Buildings - Genesis and Definition

To protect himself from extremes in climate and from maraunding animals, man felt the need for shelter initially, and utilized available natural materials for construction. As society developed, the need for privacy and protection from other men have evolved walled homes, walled cities and towers. To symbolise the social status, the chief could express his power by constructing the biggest, most visible and most often the tallest or highest located structure in the settlement. Perhaps the defensive lookout towers were actually man's first tall constructions. The very tall structures were symbolic in nature. However, the ancient tall structures could not be considered prototypes for the high-rise buildings of today. The modern skyscraper was a completely new invention with almost no antecedents prior to the middle of the 19th century (Blake, 1974). Multi-storey housing was not designed as a vertical mode of urban living. Untill the use of structural steel became common and the art of modern city planning began its development, it was rather the result of simply crowding together into exiting urban places a third dimension of high-density living.[1]

Historically, the dominant building form of each culture has represented the dominating force within that culture. The same holds true for tall buildings also. The modern skyscraper originated in Chicago, a city which was economically dominant over its region. Tall buildings might be interpreted as an expression of socio-economic reality within the context of industrialization. Usually the tallest structures are office buildings. High-rise housing tends to be more prevalent in those countries where the government is the major builder and the private enterprise promotes the tall commercial buildings. However, the real era of vertical living did not come until the later half of the 19th century.

The United States of America has maintained its lead in the construction of skyscrapers. The first high-rise structure of modern times was an eleven storeyed office building of Home Life Insurance Building in Chicago in 1884. The credit for designing this first skyscraper goes to Major William L.Jenney - an architect of Chicago, U.S.A. In 1883, the Home Insurance Company of Chicago held a competition for designing of its office building and Jenney was entrusted with the work of first high-rise building of the World.[2] By the end of 19th century height of the building reached upto 100 metres. More than 100 storeyed buildings have become prevalent in U.S.A. by mid-twentieth century only. The largest structure of America is the World Trade Centre in New York. It was built by the Port Authority of New York and New Jersey in 1972. It is an amazing complex of 2 huge twin towers with 110 storeys each. The towers are standing 411.5 m. high and 21.33 m. below the ground surface. The centre is home for more than 1100 trading firms and organizations. On an average 50,000 people work in the World Trade Centre and over 80,000 persons visit the Centre daily.[3] Sears Tower in Chicago is the highest building in the World with 110 storyes and stands 444 meters high.

The high-rise building has now spread all over the World. In India, while Bombay taking lead in high-rise constructions, the trend has been started in all other major cities also.

Since the tallness is a relative term, the high-rise buildings are defined in a comparative sense in different countries. For example in a single-storey area, a five storey building will appear tall. In European countries, buildings with more than 12 storeys are generally considered tall. Whereas in central parts of Chicago or New York a building should be around 70 to 100 storyes, if it is to be tall among the immediate neighbours. Beedle (1977) groups buildings roughly into four categories according to height.[4]

1. "Walk-ups" of three or four storeys.
2. The first group of elevator buildings, ranging between five storeys and nine to twelve storeys depending upon the country.
3. A group in the range of roughly 10 to 20 storeys.
4. Those above 20 or so storeys which have considerably stronger impact on the urban environment.

Lamela (1974) observes the following criteria for defining a tall building irrespective of height or number of storeys.

1. Net density: the ratio of total floor space built to area of site built upon (FAR) is high in relation to the norm for the locality,
2. Mechanical systems, generally elevators, are employed for vertical communication, and

3. Specialised construction and management systems and techniques, different from those employed in typical low-rise construction, are used.

Because of variable factors in different societies, a common measurable definition of high-rise building cannot be universally applied.

In India, generally with 1 + 4 floors or above are considered to be called as high-rise buildings.[5] For vertical commincations mechanical elevators (lifts) are essential in these buildings. These buildings have to meet the conditions laid down by the National Building Code 1983.

As per the Multi-storeyed Building Regulations, 1981 of Municipal Corporation of Hyderabad (M.C.H.) any building more than four floors (including the groundfloor) or whose height is 15 meters or more, measured from average level of the central line of the street on which the site abuts, is classified as multi-storeyed or high-rise building and is supposed to satisfy the conditions laid down in Part-IV of N.B.C. 1983 regarding five precautions, control and extinguisher. However, the staircase rooms, life rooms, chimneys and elevated tanks above the top most floor and architectural features shall not be included in the number of floors in calculating the height of the building. The total height of such additional construction shall not exceed the average floor height of the building. As per these regulations the maximum height allowed is 30 meters.[6]

Prior to 1981 there were no special regulations for the multi-storeyed structures. As a result of the implementation of urban land ceiling act of 1976, the restrictions on the availability of land for building purpose added to the pressure on the available developed land with the increase in land prices, the demand for residential constructions which was largely in the nature of independent houses earlier, registered a very significant change in residential type of flats in multi-storeyed structures in core areas of the city. For providing office space in the commercial areas more high-rise structures have come up. The notified master plan of the city permitted a F.S.I. of 1:4 for the commercial areas.

The new trend and fast growth of multi-storeyed buildings made the planners realise that the haphazard development of these buildings was exceeding the absorption capacity of the central core from the point of view of traffic, water supply, sanitation, fire-fighting and other basic city services. Therefore, in the larger interest of the society, it was decided to frame special measures for regulating the various aspects concerning the location, construction and other safety measures to be adopted in regard to the high-rise structures. The efforts made by HUDA and MCH in this direction took shape in the multi-storeyed building regulations, 1981 which was approved by the Government of Andhra Pradesh.

The maximum Floor Area Ratio as per the regulations is 2.00 for residential and 2.50 for commercial buildings. These are however, modified by the Government in 1987, making it uniform for both to 1 : 1.5.

Floor Area Ratio (FAR) sometimes known as Floor Space Index (FSI) is "the quotient obtained by dividing the total covered area (plinth area) on all floors by the area of the plot."

$$\text{FAR} = \frac{\text{Total covered area of all floors}}{\text{Plot area}}$$

Absolute floor areas for different types of construction and different occupancies have a definite ratio among them. Limitation of areas and heights of buildings is achieved by specifying it in terms of Floor Area Ratio (FAR) or Floor Space Index (FSI).

For Hyderabad city the FSI fixed by the corporation was very high earlier though it is 1 : 1.5 presently. Even this can be relaxed for special cases by the Municipal and Urban Development Authority upto 1 : 2. The Ministry of Municipal Administration has the previlege of granting exemptions above that also. Hence the buildings constructed earlier have the higher Floor Area Ratio. The exact Floor Area Ratios were not calculated as the correct data was not available. However, the general observation is made that the old buildings have higher ratios without giving proper importance to the parking and open spaces.

High-rise Buildings - Essential Amenities

High-rise buildings which create high density in the area should be constructed by taking extra care on some aspects. Building should provide adequate parking facilities to its inhabitants. If the buildings is for residential purpose, the open spaces should be provided for, apart from parking, children's playground, garden, etc. In view of the large number of business houses, families, servants, visitors, etc. in a high-rise buildings certain amenities are essential and must be planned right from the beginning. These amenities would make staying in high-rise buildings more comfortable. Security, saftey and providing elevators for vertical communication are some important issues to be considered carefully while planning the building.

Advantages and Disadvantages of HRBs

High-rise buildings have been the subject of controversy for their utility. The height has always fascinated man. He has dreamt of building higher and higher. They attract the visitor and boost the economic status of the city. A high-rise building is a status symbol of a city.

On the other hand criticism is levelled against these buildings as vertical castles, filing cabinets, pegion holes, vertical slums and so on. These are also imagined as crimes against humanity in view of the pshychological problems created amongst residents therein.

Therefore, as in many cases, the subject of high-rise buildings is also divided between two schools of thoughts. Some favour the idea of skyscrapers while others do not agree on this point. Some of the advantages and disadvantages are as follows:

Advantages:

1. High-rise buildings accommodate large number of families and business houses.
2. Important Locations: As the commercial development rises to peak in the urban core, more and more people like to have their offices and houses in central areas, which leads to high demand for the land in these areas. The movement in the third dimension will satisfy the rising situation.
3. They reduce the distance to be travelled by the occupants, thereby saving in travel time, cost and energy.
4. They permit more open spaces around the buildings and this open space can be used for various purposes such as play grounds, parks, and recreation, etc.
5. They provide more sunlight and pure air to the residents and gives them relief against noise nuisance.
6. Vertical expansion results in curtailment of costs of various services such as water supply, transport, electrification and drainage, etc.
7. High-rise buildings save precious land which can be utilized for agricultural and industrial purposes.
8. These are more remunerative or paying proportions.
9. They provide conveniences such as offices, markets and other amenities in the same buildings.
10. The staying on upper floors grants the pleasure of scenic views of near and distant objects, such as man-made and natural objects.

Disadvantages

1. The construction cost increases as height increases on account of services such as elevators, fire fighting devices, water

supply, drainage, garbage disposal, etc. The structural cost also goes up as the extra strength is to be provided to the building and the cost of vertical transportation of building materials and labour increases in proportion to the height.

2. The recurring cost of maintaining the necessary common services in the building will be more compared to low rise buildings.
3. It becomes difficult for children and old people to undertake vertical travel when lift or elevator fails. The children are likely to have psychological problems as the parents fear to send their children downstairs for playing.
4. The benefit of enjoying the charm of private garden cannot be obtained by the residents.
5. If located improperly and without any planning with respect to the surrounding features of the area, a high-rise may spoil the skyline of a city. It may deprive the sunlight and air of others.
6. It is quite likely that a high-rise may cause an obstructions to air traffic and micro-wave transmissions.
7. There is considerable increase in the land value due to the construction of high-rise buildings and it ultimately necessitates into the constructions of more tall buildings.
8. Always there is fear of panic in cause of emergency such as fire or earthquake, etc.
9. The studies have revealed that as building height increases, crimes increase in interior public spaces i.e. within the compound of the large high-rise residential colonies. One can list out many other reasons agianst and in favour of vertical expansion. However their necessity and optimum planning will enrich the skyline of a city.

Spatial patterns of High-rise Buildings

The urban core is a highly dynamic zone which is very unstable as low density areas are constantly converted to high-density. The high-rise development is closely associated with many factors like land values, accessibility, availability of buildable land, and location of Government offices. The government policies regulating these development also influence to large extent.

The spatial distribution of high-rise buildings (Table 3.1) give a clear account of the influence of above factors.

TABLE 3.1 : Hyderabad City: Distribution of High-rise Buildings — City Zone wise, 1991

S. No.	City Zone	No. of High-rise buildings
1.	Hyderabad South	6
2.	Hyderabad North	120
3.	Secunderabad	28
	Total -	154

Source: Field work

Hyderabad South though it registers a high density of population the vertical growth is not getting any prominence in this zone. This is the oldest part of the city, and mostly a static one both in spatial and economic point of view. Only six high-rise building blocks are found in this area.

On the other hand the Hyderabad North and Secunderabad is experiencing fast and continuous high-rise growth (fig 3.1). This may be due to the location of more government and private offices. The dual commercial core of the city also lies respectively in the centre of these zones.

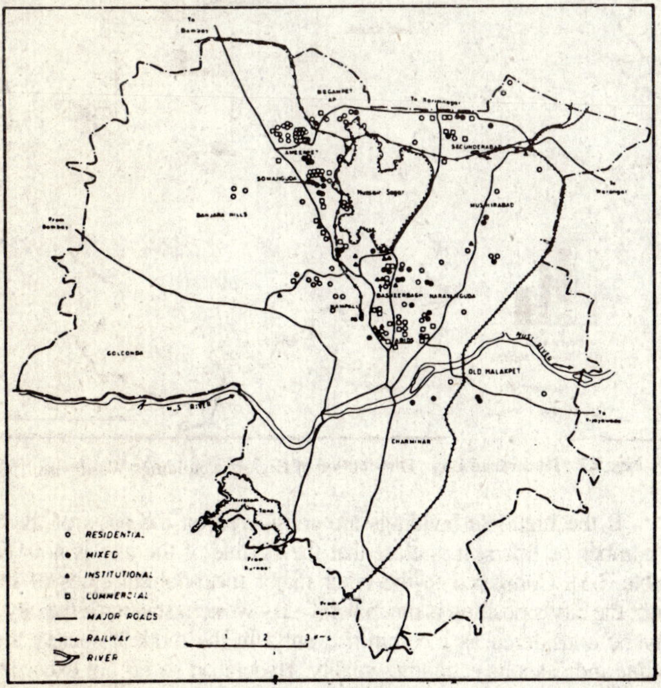

Fig. 3.1 : Hyderabad City : High-rise Buildings, 1981

Further it has been found that the distribution at micro-level (fig. 3.2 and Table 3.2) more high-rise buildings are along the main road from Abids to Secunderabad. Sixth ward, inspite of its medium density of population has grown vertically more because of more office locations and higher land values.

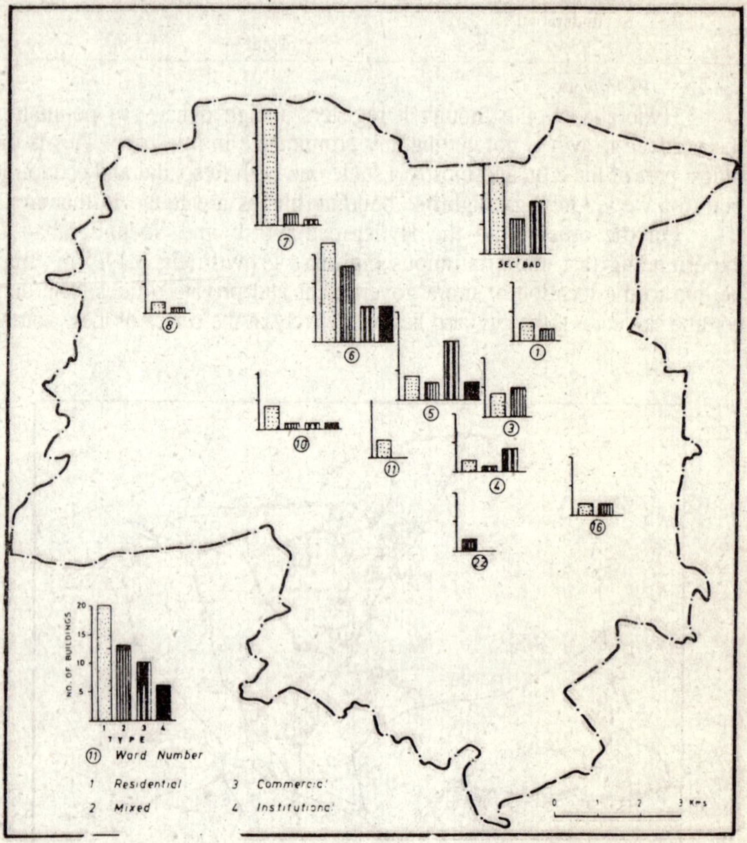

Fig. 3.2 : Hyderabad City : Distribution of High-rise buildings-Ward-wise, 1991

If the high-rise buildings are considered on the basis of their height or number of floors, it is clear that the skyline of the city is not very high (Table 3.3). Compared to the other major metropoliran cities of India, no doubt the city's position is much below. By western standards the city skyline may be considered as medium-rise only. In the modern society the city's skyline indicates its economic vitality. Hyderabad so far not exceeded more than 15 floors, for its commercial buildings, whereas twelve floor structures are highest among residential high-rise. There are just four units which have more than 10 floors. A glance at the table below gives an overall picture of the city's skyline. Eight floor structures are to be considered as the average high-rise buildings in the city.

TABLE 3.2 : Hyderabad City: Distribution of High-rise Buildings-Ward wise, 1991

Ward Number	No. of High-rise Buildings				Total
	Residential	Commercial	Mixed	Institutional	
Hyderabad					
1	3	1	2	-	6
3	4	-	5	-	9
4	2	4	1	-	7
5	4	10	3	3	20
6	17	6	13	6	42
7	20	1	2	-	23
8	2	-	1	-	3
10	4	1	1	1	7
11	3	-	-	-	3
16	2	-	2	-	4
22	-	-	2	-	2
Secunderabad	13	9	6	-	28
Total -	74	32	38	10	154

Source: Field work

TABLE 3.3 : Hyderabad City: Distribution of High-rise Buildings based on Number of Floors, 1991

S. No.	No. of floors	City Zone			Total
		Hyderabad South	Hyderabad North	Secundrabad	
1.	5 - 6	1	23	10	34
2.	7 - 8	1	84	11	96
3.	9 - 10	4	11	5	20
4.	11 - 12	-	1	2	3
5.	13 - 15	-	1	-	1
	Total -	6	120	28	154

Source: Field work

Usually in any city the commercial buildings stand tall among the rest and more often grow from a private enterprise. Babukhan Estate, a commercial high-rise is the highest in the city which creates more office and commercial space in the core commercial centre, Basheerbagh, of the city.

Functional Types of High-rise Buildings: Growth Distribution

Like other buildings, high-rise buildings also can be classified into several functional categories based on their use. For this study, the high-rise buildings are identified into the following categories.

1. Residential
2. Commercial
3. Mixed
4. Institutional

The distribution of high-rise buildings based on use is shown in Table 3.4 (Fig. 3.3) by city zone. Residential use of these buildings is predominant in Hyderabad North, followed by Secunderabad area. Comparatively the high-rise residential construction is very less in the city. However, the population housed in apartments is considerable. In most of the cases the vertical expansion of the residential units is limited to four floors, generally known as apartments. This may be due to the development and regulations of the buildings. In most of the cases the high-rise residential units in the city are just double than the apartment buildings in number of the floors. Pure residential high-rise units are located beside the main roads in well developed localities.

TABLE 3.4 : Hyderabad City: Distribution of High-rise Buildings Based On Use, 1991

Use	No. of High-rise Buildings			Total
	Hyderabad South	Hyderabad North	Secunderabad	
1. Residential	2	56	13	71
2. Commercial	-	22	9	31
3. Mixed	4	32	6	42
4. Institutional	-	10	-	10
Total -	6	120	28	154

Source: Field work

Commercial high-rise buildings, most of which have developed recently are along the main roads of the city. These are located in the commercial centres of Hyderabad North and Secunderabad. Out of total existing 31 complexes, 22 are in Hyderabad and 9 are found in Secunderabad.

Some high-rise buildings are put to mixed use both residential and commercial purposes. Usually the ground and first floors are being used by small commercial units, shops and the upper floors are for residential purpose. One way the residents will benefit from the basic general provisions within the same building and in other way it may also cause sufficient disturbance because of traffic and customers. Out of 120 buildings, 32 buildings in Hyderabad North are in mixed use. But the double use buildings are very few in Secunderabad area.

Lastly the buildings for institutional purpose are very few in the city, as the government is not a major builder in our country. On the whole there are 10 units which are in Hyderabad North.

The growth of high-rise buildings for the last twenty years is shown in Table 3.5. During 1971-75 there are only nine buildings out

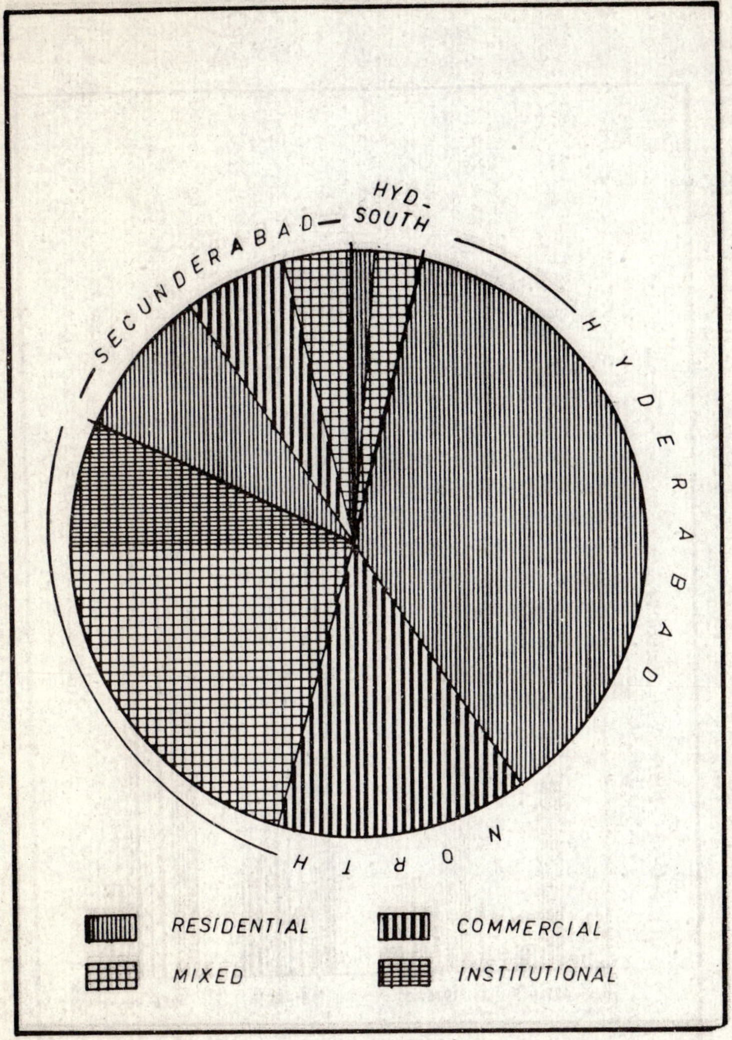

Fig. 3.3 : Hyderabad City : Distribution of High-rise buildings (Based on their use)

of which 8 are residential and one for mixed use. In the next five year period altogether 25 buildings have come up among which there are three commercial buildings. The real growth in commercial high-rise is since 1981 and accelerated for the last six years. The residential and mixed high-rise growth is steady for the last ten years. Fig. 3.4 illustrates the high-rise growth for different uses in different periods.

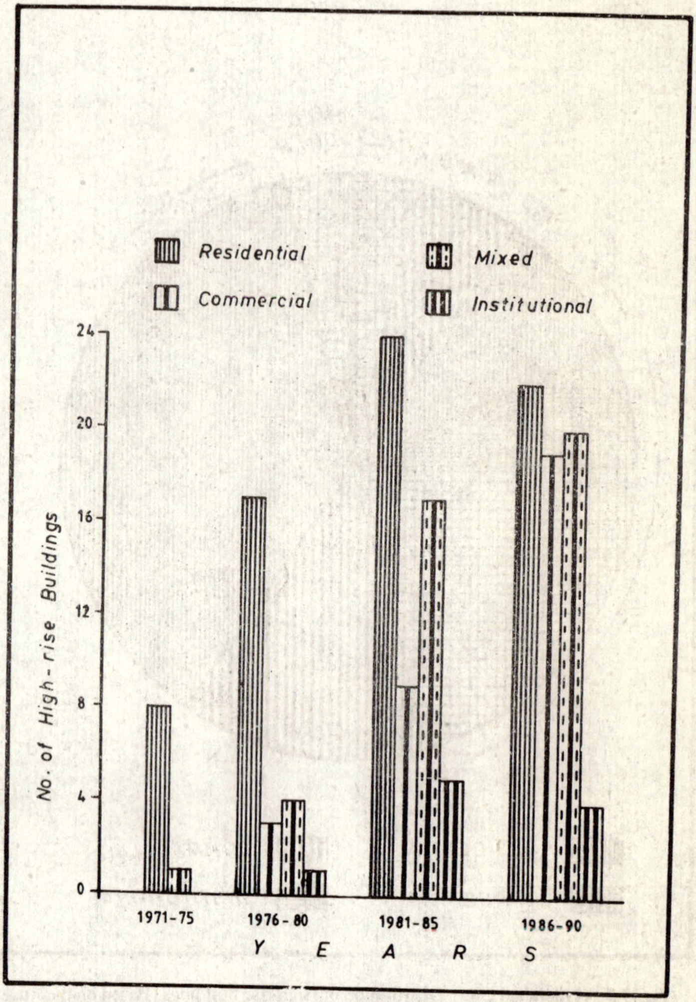

Fig. 3.4 : Hyderabad City : Growth of High-rise buildings, 1971-90

Impact of High-rise Buildings on the Morphology of the City

The High-rise development changes the city landscape and skyline. At every other street corner the twin cities seem to sprout new building projects adding new multi-storeyed commercial complexes, shopping malls and residential apartments. To accommodate the im-

TABLE 3.5 : Hyderabad City: Growth of High-rise Buildings, 1971-91

Year	No. of High-rise Buildings				Total
	Resedential	Commercial	Mixed	Institutionsl	
1971-75	8	-	1	-	9
1976-80	17	3	4	1	25
1981-85	24	9	17	5	55
1986-90	22	19	20	4	65
Total	71	31	42	10	154

Source: Field work

minent in flow of the population, the city has to increase its space to live and work within the available land. This addition of new space changes its structure in the form and to some extent function also.

As the density of population increased in the inner wards to higher levels the percent landuse for residential purposes has also been increased from time to time (Table 3.6 and Fig. 3.5). During the last two decades this change in landuse is more noticeable. It is observed that the percent of residential land during 1990 was 70.75 leaving just 3.75 per cent of land as vacant (Muzamil). During 1976 the residential land of the city was found to be 34.7 per cent and vacant land 26.5 per cent. This indicates the tremendous change in the landscape of inner city. The increase in the number of high-rise buildings during this period (Table 3.5) reveals the change in the skyline of the city.

TABLE 3.6 : Hyderabad City: Landuse, 1968-90

S. No.	Category	Percent Proportion		
		1968	1976	1990
1.	Residential land	13.4	34.7	70.75
2.	Agricultural land	17.8	9.0	2.35
3.	Transport & communication	6.7	3.4	1.70
4.	Industrial	1.6	5.2	2.05
5.	Water Bodies	7.7	5.7	5.85
6.	Vacant	39.2	26.5	3.75
7.	Others	13.6	15.5	13.55
	Total	100.00	100.00	100.00

Source:

1. Integrated Development Plan of Hyderabad, HUDA, 1979
2. Report on Optimal Development of Hyderabad, Indian Institute of Economics, Sponsored by HUDA, 1979
3. IRS IA LISS II FCC (Estimated by S. Muzamil)

The redevelopment process in the city accelerated the commercial activity in the dual central parts of the twin cities. It is also observed that the Hyderabad South has not experienced much differrence either in the form or in function in the recent periods. However, some road

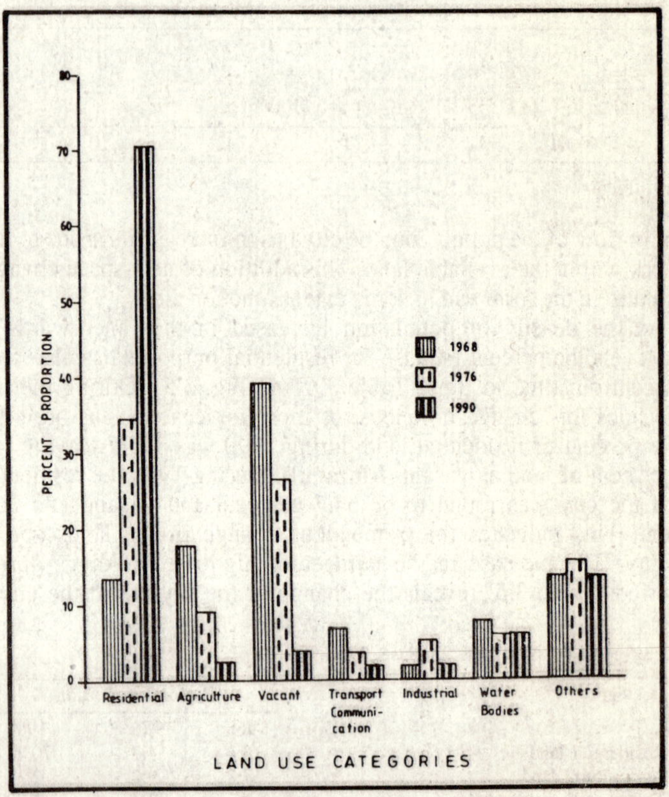

Fig. 3.5 : Hyderabad City : Land Use, 1968-1990

widening programmes were undertaken as part of redevelopment programmes by Quli Qutub Shah Urban Development Authority, which was established for the development of old city areas.

The vertical expansion of the city, as a process of redevelopment, was gradual and limited. The new multi-storeyed regulations controlled the high-rise growth in some areas as the government identified some areas not to allow for vertical growth (Fig. 3.6). Keeping in view the saturated densities and more strain on civic amenities, restrictions are imposed to prevent further developments in these areas. But it is observed that many high-rise structures are coming up in the areas of restricted zones also. This clearly indicates the laps on part of Municipality in implementing the guidelines formulated by the Hyderabad Urban Development Authority.

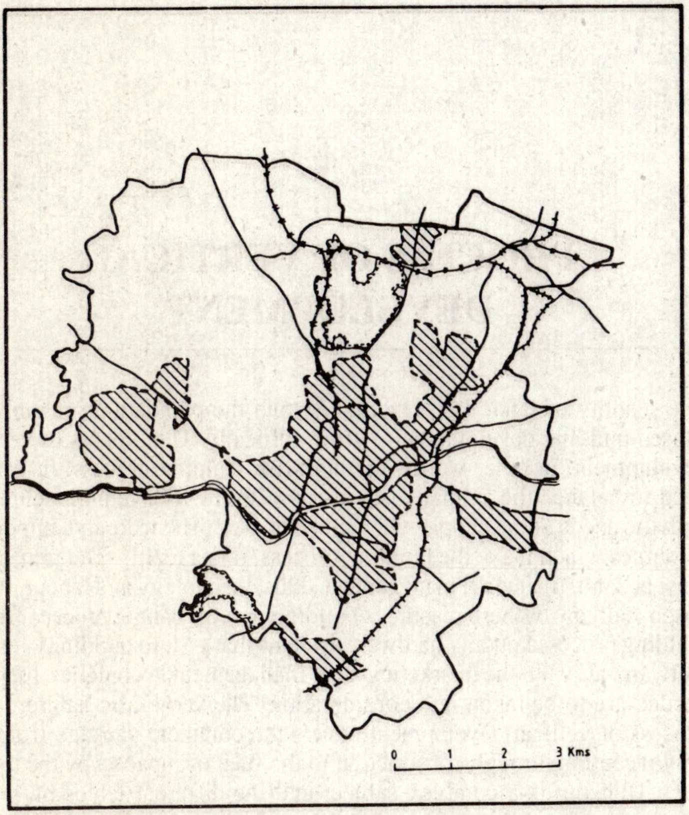

Fig. 3.6 : Hyderabad City : Multi-storeyed Buildings—Restricted Zones

REFERENCES

1. Council on Tall Buildings, Group PC, 1981, Planning and Environmental Criteria for Tall Buildings, Volume PC of Monograph on Planning and Design of Tall Buildings, ASCE, New York
2. S.C. Rangwala, "Town Planning", Charotur Publishing House, Anand, 1987
3. Ibid
4. Lynn S.Beedle (ed), Philosophy of Tall Buildings, ASCE, New York, 1981
5. National Building Code, 1983, Indian Standards Institute
6. Multi-storeyed Building Act, 1981, HUDA.

4

PROCESS OF VERTICAL DEVELOPMENT

The scarcity of land, high land values and the population pressure has caused building development to grow vertically. The process of vertical development, in other words, the high-rise building process, fulfils the need to balance the available resources with the user requirements, i.e. with the needs of the people who will be housed. There are five important resources which make the building process, into a reality. To build, there must be land, financing, management skills, technology and labour. In the absence of any of these resources building process cannot proceed. In the building process not only hardware systems that go into buildings, but the software as well the marketing and management techniques that are needed are to be taken into consideration. The very basic nature of the process of vertical development covers the complete package from the very inception through construction to the final occupation by the user.

Housing is a complex subject and the different lables by which housing has been identified - by programme, by purpose or by type, i.e. low-rise or high-rise tend to complicate more the subject. Generally tall building projects may be part of redevelopment or urban renewal programmes and in most of the cases the demolition is a part of the process. Usually, they may be for a highly specialized purpose or for housing middle income families or for the rich. In the developing countries often these are located in the central parts or in areas of economic importance. Hyderabad city is no exception to this type of building activity. Whatever may be the purpose and location of the building it should never be forgotten that the building is a shelther designed primarily for healthy, decent and comfortable living. Here an attempt has been made to assess the vertical development process in the city by surveying the field and interviewing the people involved in the process.

Organizational Structure of Builders

The building activity in Hyderabad city is in the hands of both private and public agencies. But the construction of high-rise buildings is undertaken mostly by the private builders. Since the vertical development is of recent origin the government is not in favour of high-rise high density building. The part played by government agencies is the development of high-rise is very limited. However, the midrise high density apartment building activity is encouraged and developed mostly by the government agencies.

The private builders are playing major role in addition and improvement of the housing stock, both residential as well as commercial units. In twin cities, there are about 150 builders and engineers engaged in construction of high-rise buildings, directly employing hundreds of technically qualified persons like architects, engineers and surveyors and thousands of skilled, semi-skilled and unskilled labourers. However, the growth is not keeping pace with the demand, at present this private unorganised sector is the major contributor to housing stock of the city. The conversion of old bunglows and buildings with huge open courtyards or gardens into the high density vertical complexes is undertaken by private builders with the motivation of getting profits in this real estate business.

TABLE 4.1 : Hyderabad City: Nature of Builders, 1991

Nature	Number of Builders	Percent
Individuals	20	35.00
Private Limited Companies	34	60.00
Public Institutions	3	5.00
Total	57	100.00

Source: Field work

The data on Table 4.1 (Fig. 4.1) is obtained from the sample survey of the builders in the city, gives an understanding on the involvement of different builders engaged in construction activity and their relative contributions.

As per the sample data collected at the existing construction sites, the individual builders engaged in this activity are 35 percent. Individuals may construct for self or business purpose. But builders under the category of Private Limited Company who constitutes to 60 per cent of total builders, develop the buildings only for sale. However, these first two categories are the part of private sector and together they are the chief agents for developing the building activity in the central parts of the city. Hyderabad has largely seen only public agencies involved in house building activity during past. Private agen-

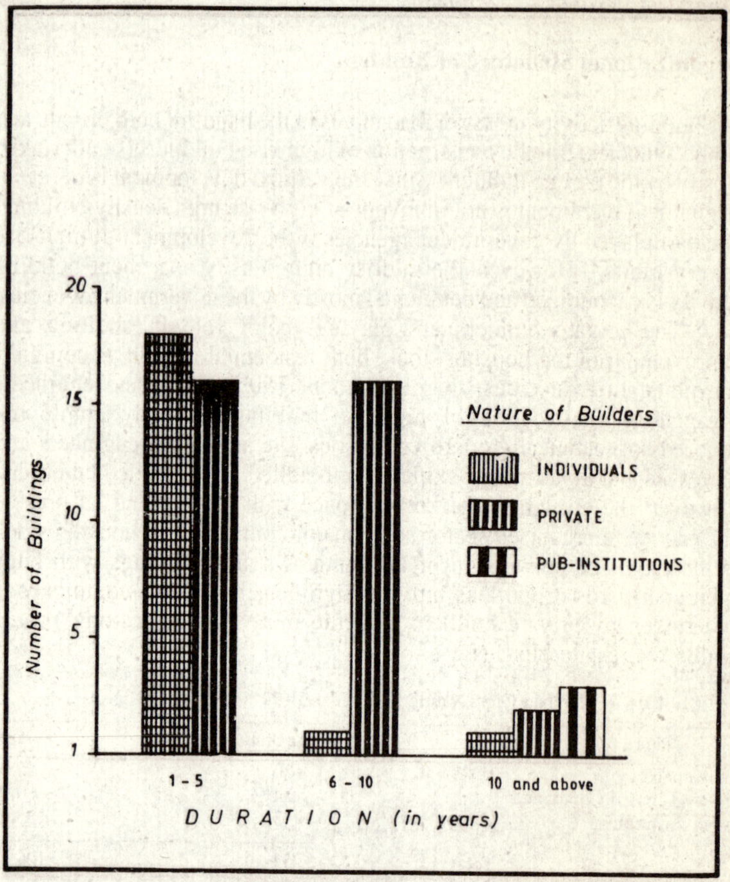

Fig. 4.1 : Nature of Builders and their duration of Business, 1991

cies entered the picture after financial institutions started financing housing projects and schemes. The role of government institutions is meagre in these areas as their sites are mostly out of the city limits. Usually government institutions concentrate on big projects and for this they need large open areas, presently which is difficult to find.

The existing Housing Acts, Codes and Regulations are not providing any powers to these institutions to acquire private land in the dilapidated and arrested areas of inner parts of the city. As such only the individuals and private agencies can actively participate in promoting housing in developed parts of the city. The Hyderabad Urban Development Authority (HUDA) and Andhra Pradesh Housing Board (APHB) are the two important government institutions in addition to the Municipal Corporation of Hyderabad (MCH) which promote the building activity in the city. Though there are no incidences that these institutions have developed the high-rise residential buildings in the city, they constructed the high-rise commercial complexes creating more office space and for commercial and shopping units. It is strange that the authorities are not realising the necessity of high-rise residential growth to meet the accute shortage and relieve congestion.

The private builders have become more in number during the recent period. As the demand for housing units in central parts is increasing immensely, more private agencies are coming forward to take advantage of the situation. The duration of their business in this field, reveals the growth and intensity of the private developers in the city (Table 4.2).

TABLE 4.2 : Hyderabad City: Period of Building Activity of Builders, 1991

Years in Business	Number of Builders	Percent
1 - 5	34	60.00
6 - 10	17	30.00
Above 10	6	10.00
Total	57	100.00

Source: Field work

Sixty per cent of the existing builders have started their business within the last five years and thirty percent are having the experience from six to ten years. This might be due to the reason that people may not understand the business properly as it depends on many changing factors. The builders who understand the building activity and succeed in developing and managing the real estate are likely to stay in the business.

Investment Pattern and Structure in High-rise Buildings

As discussed earlier land is the most important factor in the building activity. The scarcity of land in the inner parts of the city will result in higher land values. In fact the rising land value and increasing demand for built up space is an impetus for high-rise development. Unit cost of built up space is much cheaper and this leads to vertical land development. It may be noted that a flat in high-rise buildings costs much less than an independent house of same size at the same locality.

The vacant land in the inner areas is getting exhausted and the old structures have to be pulled down to redevelop the area with more living space. Presently the high-rise building activity is both on open land and on sites after demolishing old structures (Table 4.3). Both are almost in same proportion presently. But in future the developers may have to depend on old low-rise structures by inducing the owners with higher payments for their projects, as the open spaces are diminishing at faster rates in the inner city.

The relative cost effectiveness is the most important factor in promoting high-rise building projects. Family accommodation in high-rise building is much cheaper compared to single dwelling units of comparable space and quality. The total outlay of high-rise projects is usually high and the project is started with initial investment by the builder. The ultimate investment is by individual owners, who are assisted by financial institutions by granting liberal loans.

TABLE 4.3 : Hyderabad City: Nature of Site for High-Rise Building Projects, 1991

Site developed on		Number of Units	Percent
Open land (Vacant land)		29	50.9
Site after demolishing old building		28	49.1
	Total	57	100.00

Source: Field work

The responses received on the investment pattern on high-rise buildings in Hyderabad city are given in Table 4.4 (Fig. 4.2). This sample covers only units under construction presently. For some of the commercial projects the promoters are maintaining ownership and they invest with the help of financing agencies. When they intend to sell the units, cost is paid in a phased manner by the purchaser. Even the promoters are providing facility to the purchasers to obtain finance by mortgaging the unit subject to some conditions.

TABLE 4.4 : Hyderabad City: Initial Investment Pattern in High-Rise Building Project, 1991

Investor		Average percent share of initial investment
Owners of individual flats/Units or purchasers		38.0
Builders/Developers		29.5
Financing Agencies		32.5
	Total	100.00

Source: Field work

It is observed that the investment on the high-rise project before its completion is borne by different sources. Major portion (38%) of the investment is covered by the customers or purchasers who planned to own the units. The developers and financing agencies are sharing the cost of the project on average 30 and 32 per cent of total cost

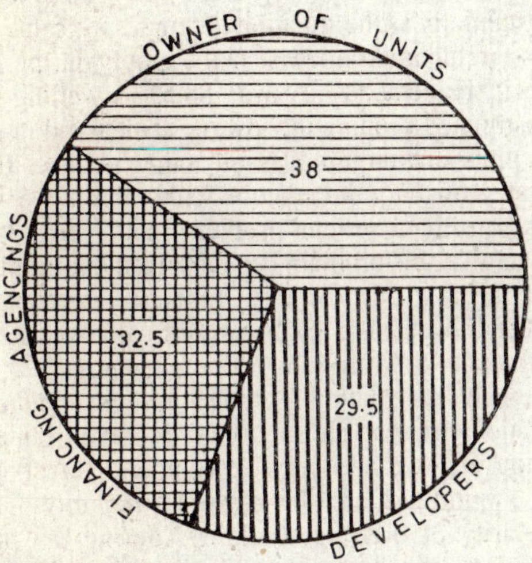

Fig. 4.2 : Investment Pattern in High-rise Building Project, 1991

respectively. This pattern may vary for different projects. However, it is the owners, who finally bear the cost of the project.

It may be seen from data on Table 4.5 that 86 per cent of the owners of space in high-rise buildings have made one time payment before taking possession of the units. Just 14 per cent of the owners have opted for payment by easy instalment over longer periods of time even after the occupation of the units.

TABLE 4.5 : Hyderabad City: Sale of Units in High-rise Buildings, 1991

Mode of Payment	Number of responses	Percent
One time payment (Before occupying the Flats/Units)	49	86.0
Instalment basis	8	14.0
Total	57	100.00

Source: Field work

Housing Situation in Hyderabad City and Growth of High-rise Buildings

In Hyderabad city, as is elsewhere in the country, construction has failed to keep pace with the increased demand for housing units. According to 1981 census there are 3,41,499 occupied residential houses as against 4,37,452 households in Hyderabad city, and by now these figures might have gone up substantially as the situation continues the same until today. Though there was a tremendous increase in the supply during 1971-81 the housing shortage in Hyderabad city was 88,513 dwelling units as of 1981.[1] It is also estimated keeping in view the same trend in supply, that 77,000 dwelling units are required as on today to meet the existing shortage. The fast growth of population without relative increase in dwelling units is causing a serious problem in the city. It would be unrealistic to expect that this problem can be solved overnight.

The vacant lands within the city limits are decreased to large extent and to meet the existing shortage vertical expansion by constructing multi-storeyed buildings should be encouraged.

In the modern World, there is a tendency to grow more and more vertical. In all major cities single or double storeyed buildings have become uncommon and we see only skyscrapers. Infact, beautifully designed high-rise buildings are the pride of any city. The sudden growth and popularity of high-rise buildings during the past decade have given an absolute new look to the twin cities of Hyderabad and Secunderabad.

People, usually, misunderstand the grwoth of high-rise buildings as they cause high density of population, increasing the congestion in traffic and causing strain on the existing water supply, electricity and drainage systems. This is purely a misconception and nothing to do with high-rise buildings. The local municipalities permit them after satisfying the Floor Space Index (FSI). When the ratio of permissible floor area remains constant, it can be achieved either by spreading more on the ground or by going more and more vertical to save valuable land which can be utilised for better wide roads, parking, parks and play grounds, etc. From environmental point of view more open space is desirable.

The Role of Real Estate Agents and Institutions in Developing High-rise Buildings

Generally in metropolitan housing markets the real estate agents and building societies assist in the sale of residential and commercial units. Though the developers go for a reasonable publicity, it is the agents who contact personally the buyer and prepare them mentally to go for the purchase. These agents are normally compensated by the seller on the basis of a commission that is a fixed percentage of the sale price or lumpsum amount on each unit. It has long been common practice in the housing market for sellers of dwelling units to retain real estate agents or brokers to give publicity and sell their units.

On the other hand the building societies and financial institutions help the buyer in financing the purchase of units thus promoting the sale indirectly. The situation in high-rise buildings is the same as is elsewhere in the housing market.

In Hyderabad city agents role in real estate transactions is not-less-than elsewhere in the country. The local housing markets can be divided into two segments; dwelling units sold through real estate agents and those sold by owners directly. The survey by the author revealed that agents assist in the sale of about 42 per cent of high-rise building units in the city (Table 4.6).

TABLE 4.6 : Hyderabad City: Mode of Sale of Units in High-Rise Buildings, 1991

Sale effected		Number of respondents	Percent
Direct deal with the buyers		33	57.9
Through Agents		24	42.1
	Total	57	100.00

Source: Field survey

High-rise living in the city is not yet popular and consequently high-rise residential units are not much in demand. The new builders and developers are adopting the direct approach of individual buyers by using their personal contacts in the society. This may be the reason for larger proportion (58%) of sale made directly to the parties. In most of the cases the agents or brokers deal with both buyers and sellers and it is reasonable to expect that both the price and demand will be different in the broker-assisted segment.

The mode of sale depends upon the value and demand position of the units. The location is the chief factor in making the demand high, as the high-rise building space is usually provided in the most developed and central localities. The design and facilities provided are important factors in marketing and obtaining high value per unit. If the residential units in these buildings are not within the reach of the people for whom it is designed, the marketing becomes difficult where the role of agents and financial institutions becomes effective. Table 4.7 gives data on the demand position of high-rise building units in the city.

The demand position of the high-rise building units is considered to be moderate in the city. Usually people does not change their traditional living abode, individual separate house, unless the situation

TABLE 4.7 : Hyderabad City: Demand Positions of the Flats/Shopping Units in High-Rise Buildings, 1991

Demand Position	Number of respondents	Percent
Heavy demand	13	22.5
Moderate demand	34	60.0
Less demand	10	17.5
Total	57	100.00

Source: Field work

compels them. The space problem is likely change their option in the near future. It is hoped that if the problems of the inhabitants in these units are solved completely the demand in future for the high-rise may rise remarkably. However, there is reason to believe that the demand of high-rise residential units is quite encouraging. But the demand for commercial space in high-rise buildings is not upto the expectations of the builders. Many builders/developers have expressed their difficulty in the disposal of or renting out commercial units. This problem has been discussed in detail elsewhere in the study.

The actual role of real estate agents or brokers in the marketing of high-rise residential units has not been examined for want of empirical evidence. But the real estate agents appear to be salesmen for the housing industry and to generate effects very similar to that of advertising. The high-rise buildings do need the help of agents as well as building societies and financial institutions to reach the potential low and higher income groups.

Problems faced by the Builders

Often the builder, being the manufacturer of the building aims at giving the people what they want within the limits of what they are willing to spend. Usually before designing a high-rise building the builder thinks about the marketability of the product. High-rise building flats are generally preferred by the upper middle income group people. Balance has to be maintained, while keeping in view the necessities of those people, in designing and making provisions. In the process of developing the project, which starts from the land acquisitions to the final disposal of the individual units, the builder has to face so many problems for success of the venture. For a successful project of high-rise building, one has to have an effective demand, appropriate location, appropriate amenities and reasonable cost.

As discussed earlier the building system depends mainly on the following resources. (i) Land availability, (ii) Finance, (iii) Management skills, (iv) Technology, and (v) Labour. One way or the other the problems of the builders are linked to these resources. Apart from these resources, the functional difficulties of the process are also important.

In Hyderabad city, though the construction activity is growing rapidly, many builders have complained of several problems in their real estate business. So many new builders are coming foward to cater to the growing need of housing as accute shortage of residential houses still persists in the city due to large continuous influx of population. But their stay in the business lasts for a short period as very soon they realise the difficulties in the system. Some of the common problems faced by the builders are listed in Table 4.8 (Fig. 4.3.). The intensity

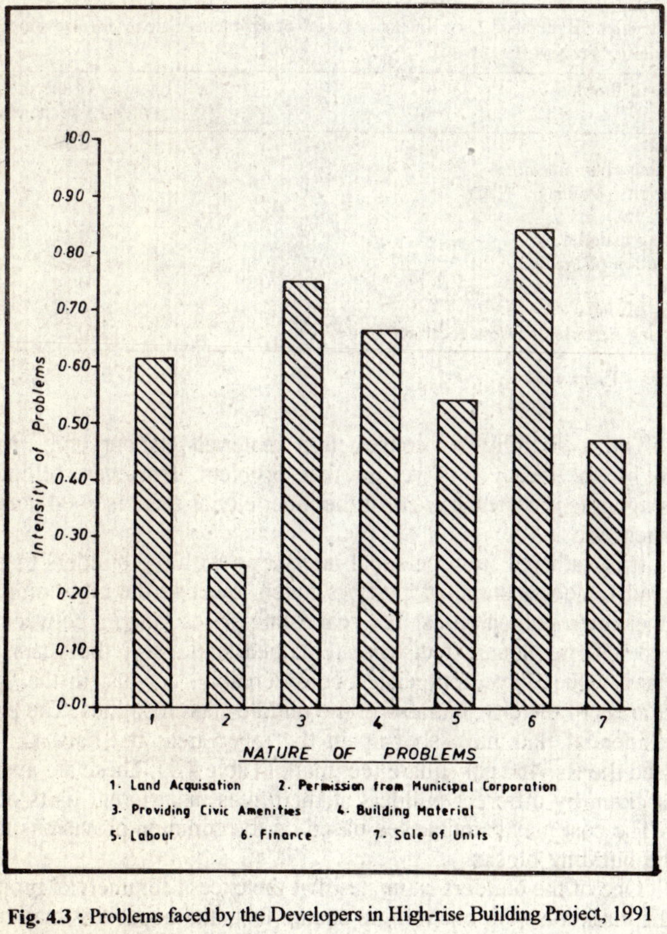

Fig. 4.3 : Problems faced by the Developers in High-rise Building Project, 1991

level of the problems is measured based on the opinion of the respondents considering the total positive response of all people as unit. Finance stands above all the problems registering 0.84 level. Out of total 57 respondents thirty five have responded positively for the difficulty in acquiring the land for a high-rise building project. Very few people have expressed difficulty in getting the municipal permission. If the builder fulfils the multi-storeyed building regulations, the permission is given without any delay. Almost 75 per cent of the developers have complained of difficulties in obtaining the provision of civic amenities like, electricity, drainage, water supply, etc.

TABLE 4.8 : Hyderabad City: Intensity Level of Problems Felt by the Developers in the Building Process, 1991

Nature of Problem	Intensity of the problem as felt by respondents
Finance	0.84
Providing civic amenities (Electricity, Drainage, Water supply, etc.)	0.75
Building material	0.67
Acquisition of land	0.62
Labour	0.54
Selling of units	0.47
Obtaining permissions from local authorities	0.25

Source: Field work

The availability of construction materials, labour and finance faced by the builders is yet another problem. However, selling of housing units is easier in areas of the inner city as there is good demand for such units.

It is gathered from personal interviews with the builders that the demand for commercial property is much lower in the city compared to other matropolitan cities. The real estate prices ranging between Rs. 250 to 350 per square feet have remained static over the years. But the land values have appreciated consideréably, not just in the upper crust areas of the city, but also in the middle class localities. The prices of residential flats have shot up in the inner areas but have still not crossed the Rs. 450 per square feet mark (Table 4.9). These are average rates given by different builders at their sites in different parts of the city. The cost may be enhanced based on the common provisions made in the building blocks.

One of the builders estimates that the excess commercial property on the market is over one million square feet, and hopes this may begin to cease or dwindle within next one or two years when propspects brighten for the city with the expected economic upswing. Some of

TABLE 4.9 : Hyderabad City: Cost of Average Plinth Area for Residential Units, 1991

Cost per square feet (Rs.)	Number of Units	Percent
225	11	19.3
250	23	40.4
275	13	22.8
300	10	17.5
Total	57	100.00

Source: Field work

the builders have expressed their unhappiness over the zonal regulations, building laws and FSI which is 1 : 1.5 presently. They pleaded for drastic changes in these rules. This was completely opposed by the planners and prospective buyers when contacted. However, most of the developers are unanimous that the State Government must take some remedial measures to put the building industry in better shape.

The overall process of vertical development is involved in many stages, right from the initiation of project proposal to the final allotment of individual high-rise units. In the process the developers have to come across the problems which are common in the building industry and specific in high-rise projects. A schematic representations of the vertical development process is given in the Fig. 4.4.

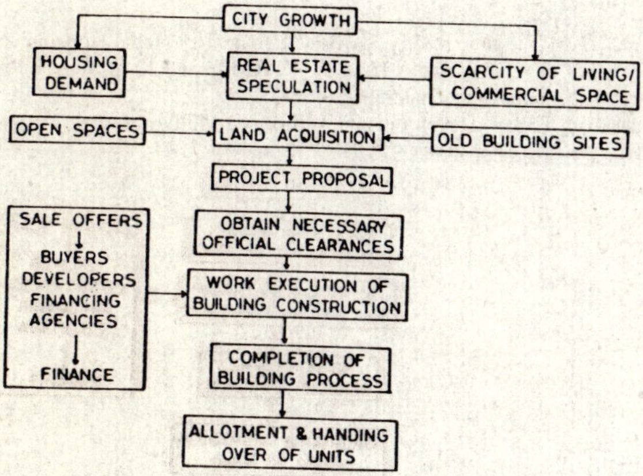

Fig. 4.4 : Vertical Development Process (Schematic)

Development Controls for High-rise Buildings

The housing process is closely related with the development controls. The zoning regulations which include various controls and norms of develop and constructions for various landuses, the building acts and regulations, the corporate stipulations, etc. will define the development controls. The development controls as such, regulate the form and content of a city.

The vertical growth of Hyderabad skyline is regulated by the multi-storeyed building act 1991.[2] The present FSI allowed in the city is 1 : 1.5 only which is very low compared to other cities in India. But it is argued that if the FSI is more there will be increase in congestion, heavy traffic and parking requirements, increase in load on services (specially water supply and power), extra cost of construction due to foundation, lifts, etc. and fire hazards. If the same floor area ratio is maintained for high-rise buildings this would facilitate more open space and would reduce the length of service networks.

In Hyderabad city due to existing high density of population, some of the areas are notified as restricted zones for high-rise development which may cause further rise in density. These areas have been shown in Fig. 3.6. The height of the high-rise construction is controlled by the norm that no building should exceed the height of 30 meters in the city. In addition to the controls and restrictions in zoning and building codes, the high- rise design should also comply with the Master Plan of the city since the high-rise construction in inner parts of the city is part of redevelopment process.

REFERENCES

1. Chary, T.M.V. and Reddy, K.N., 'Urban Housing: Housing Needs of Hyderabad city', in *Urban Crisis*, K. V. Reddy and Ram Mohan Rao (Eds.), Hyderabad publishers, Hyderabad, 1988.
2. Hyderabad Urban Development Authority, Multi-storeyed Buildings Act, 1981.

5

COMMERCIAL AND BUSINESS USE OF HIGH-RISE BUILDING SPACE

High-rise buildings have developed with the view to create more commercial space in single block within limited ground-space. The first high-rise building in the western as well as in other parts of the Wrold have been constructed for commercial use. This indicates the importance of high-rise building from the commercial point of view. The first skyscraper, built in Chicago was an Office building and the office building that is claimed to be the tallest in United States. In Indian cities like other countries, the commercial high-rise buildings stand to be tall among all others and Hyderabad is no exception to this trend.

There is a surprising similarity in the form of commercial high-rise buildings around the World. Usually the ground and first floors area in most commercial buildings is allotted for retail shopping units and the upper floors are used for office purposes.

The intensity of commercial and business space use in the central city and in its adjacent areas will be much more than in any other parts of the city. If the land use of the city for the central and adjacent areas is examined, it may be found that the proportion of land under commercial use is less, as the area is derived based on the total ground area. But if the total vertical floor space is taken into account it may be found that the commercial space account for relatively higher proportion of landuse.

The development and increase in commercial and business space in the inner city is due to upcoming high-rise structures which are part of the redevelopment process. Urban redevelopment device is a method of accelerating the natural readjustments of landuse patterns. At times re-use is specifically sought for areas peripheral to the central areas. This change or transformation is necessitated by the increase in demand for commercial and business use of space in the central parts. To cater to the ever increasing demand for office accommodation in central locations, growth in vertical dimensions is inevitable. The high-rise building space is added up in keeping pace with the value and demand from time to time.

Spatial Pattern of Space Use

In Hyderabad city the shift in the CBD and economic activity from South of Musi to the North has taken place long before the emergence of high-rise development. With the emergence of dual commercial core, one in Secunderabad and another in Hyderabad North zone, i.e. Abids, high-rise development has been taking place around these commercial cores. Many office buildings and commercial complexes are located along the main routes connecting these two cores.

The increasing demand for commercial space is perhaps confined to the CBD area, particularly, Abids and its surrounding areas. The city has its shopping heart in this areas throbbing with life till late in the night. It caters to a wide cross section of people. It is not just the haunting ground for the elite but middle class men also find their needs fulfilled. This intense commercial activity might have caused the growth of high-rise buildings just peripheral to and around Abids centre, Koti, M.J. Market, Nampally Station Road and Basheerbagh. These are the four sides of the centre where the high-rise buildings with commercial utility have come up. These areas are capable of absorbing more commercial high-rise buildings. Particularly Basheerbagh has the capacity to absorb more commercial high-rise buildings among all other areas and in coming years this area would become another nerve-centre of business and commercial activity.

A survey has been conducted on the shopping units and offices located in the commercial high-rise buildings in the city. The resultant data on Table 5.1 illustrates the size of shopping units in the high-rise complexes in the city. It is observed that the shopping units with carpet area less than 50 sq.ft. account for 50 percent of the total number of units. Thirty percent of the units are having carpet area ranging from 500 to 2000 sq.ft. The remaining units have above 2000 sq.ft. carpet area. This suggests that relatively more number of units in high-rise

TABLE 5.1 : Hyderabad City: Percent Units/Shops by Carpet Area Located in High-Rise Buildings, 1991

Carpet Area in Sq. Ft.	Number of Units	Percent
500 and less	84	50.3
501 - 2000	38	30.0
2001 - 5000	24	15.7
Above 5000	6	4.0
Total	152	100.00

Source: Field work

complexes have less carpet area perhaps due to the fact that the ground and lower floors of such buildings are provided with small retail shopping units.

The spatial distribution of the shopping and office units in high-rise buildings are shown by city zones in Table 5.2 (Fig. 5.1). The city South zone is characterized by its retail structure by accommodating small shopping units with less carpet area in case of high-rise building space. There are no commercial high-rise buildings in this zone. The ground and first floors are being used for commercial prupose and the upper floors are for residential apartments. This is the general

Fig. 5.1

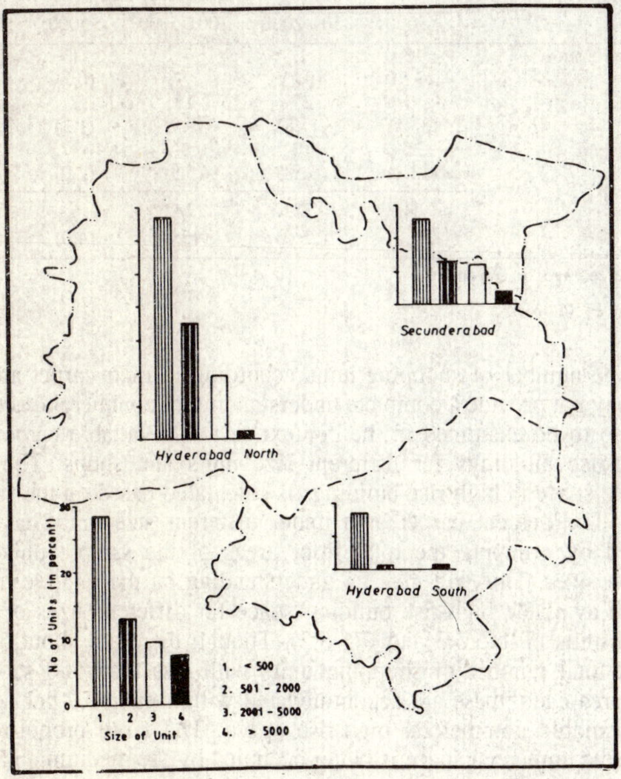

Fig. 5.1 : Zone-wise Units/Shops by Carpet Area in High-rise Buildings, 1991

pattern everywhere in case of mixed used high-rise buildings. But in the North zone and in Secunderabad apart from mixed use there are pure commercial high-rise buildings which provide more space for wholesale and office establishments. It was observed from the field survey that in case of mixed high-rise buildings the apartments, meant for residential purpose, are being used for commercial purpose by locating the offices of small business establishments, like finance companies, brokerage and training institutions. These are mostly in buildings located in the central parts and along main roads.

TABLE 5.2 : Hyderabad City: Distribution of Shops by Carpet Area and City Zones in High-Rise Buildings, 1991

City Zone	Number of Units/Carpet area in sq. ft.				
	500	501-2000	2001-5000	>5000	TOTAL
Hyderabad South	13	1	-	1	15
	(8.5)	(0.7)		(0.7)	(9.9)
Hyderabad North	51	27	15	2	95
	(33.5)	(17.8)	(9.9)	(1.3)	(62.5)
Secunderabad	20	10	9	3	42
	(13.2)	(6.58)	(5.9)	(2.0)	(27.6)
All zones -	84	38	24	6	152
	(55.2)	(25.0)	(15.8)	(4.0)	(100.0)

Note : Percentages in Parentheses.

Source: Field work

The number of shopping units according to their carpet area by itself may not provide a complete understanding of commercial activity. It is also to be examined in the context of total available carpet area in high-rise buildings for different size units and shops. The total available space in high-rise buildings is calculated based on the sample survey. The percent carpet area under different size units has been obtained by grouping the total floor areas of the sample units into different sizes. This will give an understanding on the relative importance of available high-rise building space for different sizes of commercial units (Table 5.3 and Fig 5.2). Though there are about 50 per cent of total number of shopping units with less than 500 sq.Fit of carpet area each, these are accommodated within just 11.9 per cent of total available commercial high-rise space. The large proportion of high-rise commercial space is being occupied by the medium and large establishments. Forty percent of total available space is provided for the units with 2000 to 5000 sq.ft. of carpet area each. About 24 per cent of available high-rise commercial space is being used by the units with size of 501-2000 and above 5000 sq.ft. carpet area each. An analysis of proportion of carpet area by size of units will reveal that

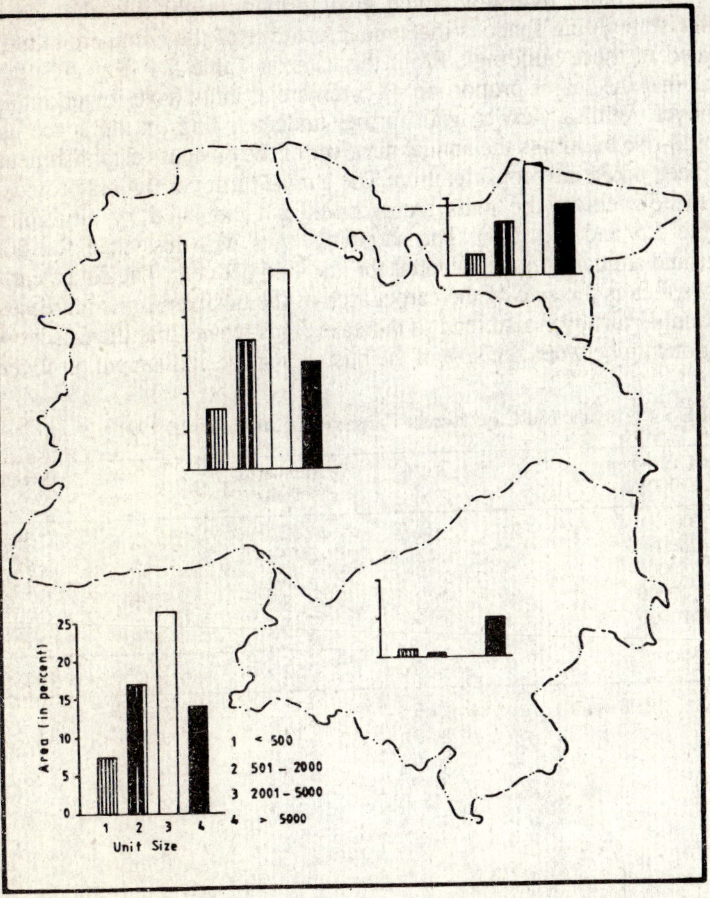

Fig. 5.2 : Zone-wise percent Carpet Area of Units/Shops in High-rise Buildings, 1991

the most of high-rise building space is created in keeping in view the large commercial units and office establishments.

TABLE 5.3 : Hyderabad City: Percent Carpet Area of Commercial Units in High-Rise Buildings by Size and City Zone, 1991

City Zone	Carpet Area is sq. Ft. (size of Units)				
	500	501-2000	2001-5000	>5000	Total
Hyderabad South	1.06	0.43	-	5.11	6.60
Hyderabad North	8.06	17.16	25.93	8.78	59.93
Secunderabad	2.78	6.99	14.51	9.19	33.47
Total -	11.90	24.58	40.44	23.08	100.00

Source: Field work

The other indicator which give further insight into the use of high-rise building space is the annual turnover of the commercial units located in these buildings. From the data on Table 5.4 (Fig. 5.3) it is clear that the major proportion of commercial units have lower annual turnover. With a view to gain further understanding on the space use in high-rise buildings the annual turnover of the business establishments has been taken into consideration. The annual turnover figures provided by the owners of the units are grouped and tabulated by city zones (Table 5.5 and Fig. 5.4). The shopping units with less than Rs. 500 thousand annual turnover account for just 4.46 per cent. The data clearly shows that as the size of the carpet area of the business units increases, the annual turnover also tend to increase. This means that there is close relationship between the size of the business space and annual turnover.

TABLE 5.4 : Hyderabad City: Percent Units by Annual Turnover, 1991

Annual Turnover (in Rs. '000)	Number of Units	Percent
Upto 500	52	34.2
501 - 2500	63	41.5
2501 - 5000	23	15.1
5001 - 10000	8	5.3
Above 10000	6	3.9
Total -	152	100.00

Source: Field work

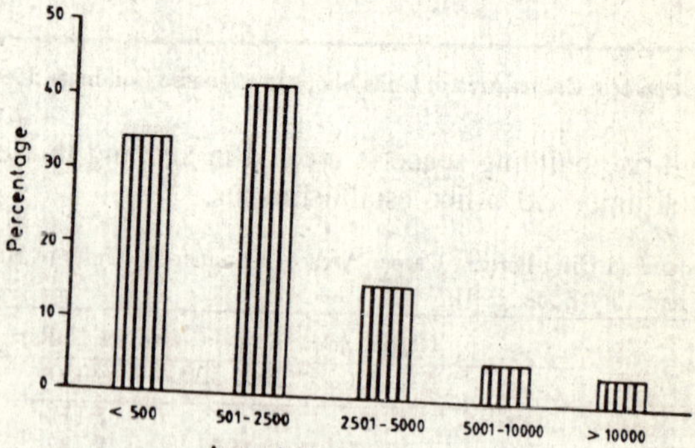

Fig. 5.3 : Percent Units by Annual turnover: High-rise Buildings, 1991

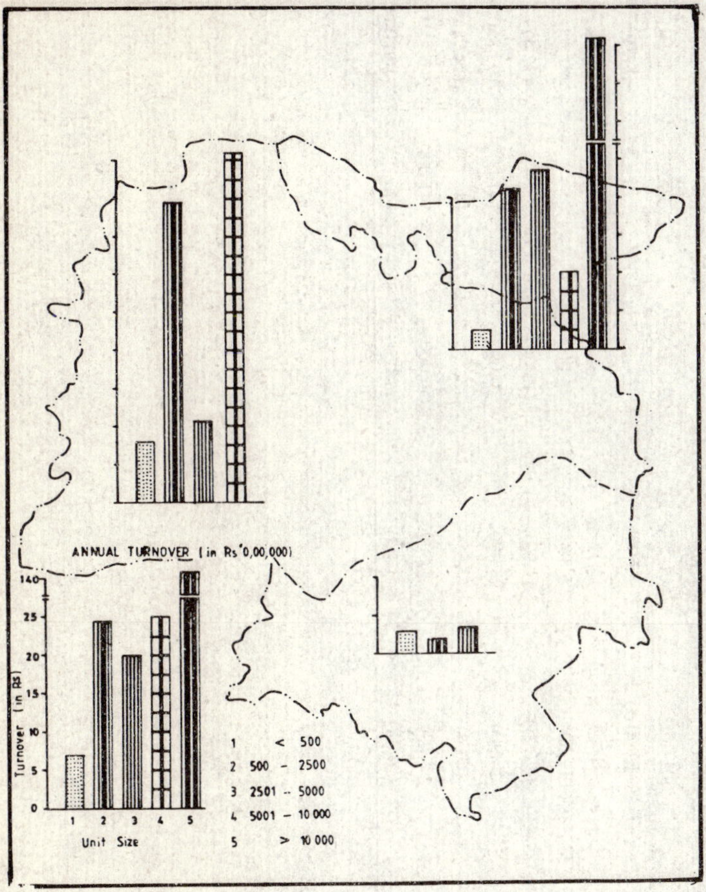

Fig. 5.4 : Zone-wise percent of Units/Shops by Annual turnover in High-rise Buildings, 1991

In order to see if there is any relationship between location and annual turnover of business units the data has been tabulated by city zones. Both location and carpet area of the business units seem to be related to the annual turnover of the units. However, the impact of carpet area on turnover varies depending on the city zone (location). Shops located in high-rise buildings in Hyderabad North has more carpet area compared to Secunderabad. But the annual turnover of shops in Secunderabad is relatively higher than Hyderabad North. This suggests the absence of clear and direct relationship between carpet area of the shop and their annual turnover in some areas.

TABLE 5.5 : Hyderabad City: Annual Turnover of Units/shops in High-Rise Buildings by City Zones, 1991

City Zone	Annual Turnover in Rs. '000					
	Upto 500	501-2500	2501-5000	5001-10000	10000	Total
Hyderabad South	3,210	1,800	3,600	-	-	8,610
	(1.05)	(0.59)	(1.18)			(2.82)
Hyderabad North	7,890	39,600	5,800	46,000	-	99,290
	(2.58)	(12.95)	(1.90)	(15.04)		(32.47)
Secunderabad	2,550	20,900	23,400	10,000	141,000	197,850
	(0.83)	(6.84)	(7.65)	(3.27)	(46.12)	(74.71)
Total -	13,650	62,300	32,800	56,000	141,000	305,750
	(4.46)	(20.38)	(10.73)	(18.3)	(46.12)	(100.00

Note: Percentages in Parentheses.

Source: Field work

The overall spatial pattern of the commercial high-rise space use exhibits a concentration of both the retail and wholesale commercial activity. However, smaller units have relatively less investment and are mostly confined to ground and first floors while the larger units with relatively large investments occupy the higher floors.

Ownership and Commercial Space Use

Commercial space is usually purchased and can be considered as an investment since it accrues good return in the form of rent to the owner. Particularly the high-rise space is either kept with the developers themselves or sold to individuals who may use it or let it on rental basis. In most of the high-rise complexes the developers also let the shopping units or floor space on long-term lease basis on monthly rent. It is observed that in case of mixed use high-rise buildings the small shopping units are sold out to individuals who may use it for shops and in some cases it is let out to others for use. However, in case of upper floors of such buildings the space is given to large establishments or government departments on lease. The rent per square foot is more in case of small units in ground and first floors, whereas it is comparatively less for upper floors space.

Of the total 152 commercial units under study about 87.5 per cent are tenants. The owership of this space is with some other people who gets monthly rents on this space. The owners who run the shopping units in their own space amount to a meagre 12.5 per cent. These figures indicate the investment pattern in commercial high-rise space. In Hyderabad South zone in some cases complete units are with tenants whereas in Hyderabad North and Secunderabad a small proportion of units are run by owners of the space (Table 5.6 and Fig. 5.5).

TABLE 5.6 : Hyderabad City: Tenure of the Commercial Units in High-rise Buildings, 1991

City zone	Owners		Tenants	
	No. of Units	Percent	No. of Units	Percent
Hyderabad South	-	-	15	10.0
Hyderabad North	13	8.5	82	54.0
Secunderabad	6	4.0	36	23.5
Total —	19	12.5	133	87.5

Source: Field work

The stability of the business in commercial high-rise buildings seem to be affected as the people tend to change their locations frequently. The duration of the business in their present existing premises is surveyed and is found that many units have not completed their initially agreed term. Perhaps this may be due to the recent

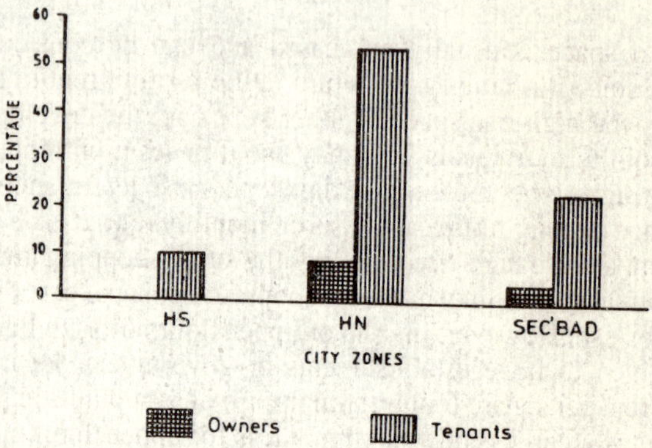

Fig. 5.5 : Tenure of the Commercial Units in High-rise Buildings, 1991

development of more and more high-rise buildings. But there are instances for units in such buildings continue in business for more than a decade also. This trend is particularly true of small shopping units.

The evidence as represented in Table 5.7 indicates that more than half of the units in high-rise buildings have short duration of less than three years in the present premises. There are hardly two per cent units which have been in the same high-rise buildings for more than 10 years. The reason for this may perhaps be the hike in rent by the owners year after year particularly in case of smaller units. Since most of the larger units using larger space are likely to be long-term lease holders and the impact of rent hike may not be very significant.

TABLE 5.7 : Hyderabad City: Number of Years of Occupancy in High-rise Complex by Units/Shops, 1991

Number of Years	Number of Units	Percent	Cumulative Percent
1 - 3	84	55.3	55.3
4 - 6	56	36.8	92.1
7 - 9	9	5.9	98.0
10 and above	3	2.0	100.0
Total —	152	100.0	100.00

Source: Field work

Rent is one of the indicators which reveal the intensity of space demand and concentration of the commercial activity in the city. As most of the high-rise complexes have been centrally located usually the rental value of space is high. It may be seen from data on Table 5.8 that unit area rent consistantly decline with the increase in carpet area of unit. The average rent per sq.ft. is Rs. 5.80 for small units with carpet area of 300 sq.ft. or less. The corresponding figures are Rs. 5.40 for units with area between 301 to 600 sq.ft. and Rs. 3.10 for units with area above 600 sq.ft. This clearly brings a direct inverse relationship between the carpet area of the commercial units and unit area rent for the space use. It is observed from the field survey that rent ranges from 5 to 20 rupees per square foot in the central areas of the city in case of smaller shopping units in the ground and first floors. The rent for the upper floors does not exceed even 6 rupees so far. Many people have consider that the rent for the commercial space in high-rise buildings in Hyderabad is very low compared to other metropolitan cities in India.

TABLE 5.8 : Hyderabad City: Average Monthly Rent Per Sq.ft. Floor Space by City Zone and Size Units, 1991

Size Units	City zones/Average Monthly Rent per square feet			Total city Rs.
	Hyderabad South Rs.	Hyderabad North Rs.	Secunderabad Rs.	
Small size units (300 sq.ft., and less carpet area)	2.80	6.60	8.10	5.80
Medium size units (301-600 sq.ft., carpet area)	2.30	6.30	7.70	5.40
Large size units (More than 600 sq. ft. carpet area)	2.00	3.20	4.20	3.10
Average of all sizes	2.40	5.35	6.65	4.75

Source: Field work

It is interesting to note the spatial pattern of rental values of commercial space in high-rise buildings, a reflection of the intensity of commercial activity and the economic dynamism of the various city zones (Table 5.8). It may be seen that Hyderabad South has the lowest per unit area rent for all sizes of commercial space and on the other extreme is Secunderabad. Hyderabad North occupy an intermediate position. One inference that can be drawn from this perhaps is that Secunderabad has relatively greater economic dynamism in so far as commercial space use is concerned. It may also be born in mind that not only some of the best exclusive commercial use high-rise complexes are located in Secunderabad but the number of such complexes are more in this city zone compared to Hyderabad South and Hyderabad North.

With a view of gain further insight into the structure of commercial space use in high-rise buildings, an opinion survey of such users was conducted and the result is presented in Table 5.9. It may be seen that a little over 54 percent of the rented commercial units consider the rent being paid by them for the space is reasonable while a little over 45 percent of them consider the rent to be high.

TABLE 5.9 : Hyderabad City: Opinion of The Commercial Space Users in High-rise Buildings, 1991

Opinion of Space Users	No. of Units	Percent
Rent is Reasonable	73	54.5
Rent is High	61	45.5
Total —	134	100.0

Source: Field work

The nature of business run in the high-rise buildings is both the retail and wholesale apart from the administrative functions. Since the skyline of the city has not been grown to higher heights it is the retail activity which dominates over the others in number. The central location of these buildings is the main determining factor for the existing pattern. Particularly it is so in case of mixed-use high-rise buildings where the shopping units are located in the ground floor. About 63 per cent of the total smaple units are the retail shops (Table 5.10) in high-rise buildings while wholesale activity accounts for about 37 per cent of the units.

TABLE 5.10 : Hyderabad City: Nature of Trade in High-Rise Buildings, 1991

Nature of Trade	No. of Units	Percent
Wholesale	56	36.8
Retail	96	63.2
Total —	152	100.0

Source: Field work

In order to assess the scale of operation of the retail trade activity in high-rise buildings, data on work-force employed by such units have been collected and is given in Table 5.11. About 41 per cent of these units employ less than five persons and 73 per cent of the units employ less than 10 persons. This means most of these units are relatively small usually owned by an individual or family run with the help of limited hired man power.

TABLE 5.11 : Hyderabad City: Number of Persons Employed in Shops/Units in High-Rise Buildings, 1991

No. of persons employed	No. of Units	Percent
1 - 5	64	40.8
6 - 10	49	32.2
11 - 20	20	13.2
21 - 40	12	7.9
41 - 100	9	5.9
Total —	152	100.0

Source: Field work

Problems and Prospects

The shortage of land at suitable locations for commercial use in central areas is the main factor for development of high-rise commercial complexes. The shortage of land, ever increasing land value and demand for space in the central parts of the city are all contributary factors in the process of high-rise building developments.

The high-rise building represent major concentrations of human activity that result in the need for more parking space. The automobile transport has developed to a large extent and in turn the vehicle traffic in the central areas grows with the commercial activity. The tall buildings as they gather more customers should provide more open space for the parking vehicles.

In Hyderabad city the high-rise structures are not planned to the full satisfaction of commercial space users. The foremost problems with these units is the insufficient parking space. Very little open spaces are provided in most cases for parking in these complexes with few exceptions of recent constructions. Many buildings are facing the main road without parking place. These are the places where large number of people visit for a variety of purposes as a variety of activities from retail trade to administrative functions are located in such buildings.

Yet another problem is the lack of proper maintenance. Many complexes are not maintained properly and also the common facilities like lift, toilet and so on are not being properly maintained.

The satisfaction of the shop keepers in the complexes with regard to the available carpet area of individual units has been examined by interviewing them. A fairly large proportion of people are satisfied with their floor space. Just 18 persons out of total 152 have indented for some more space than they are using presently. This demand for additional space requirement varies from 150 sq.ft. by smaller units to 10000 sq.ft. by large establishments.

The location of more units in a single building may cause strain on amenities provided for the shopping units. This has been listed in Table 5.12 by assessing the opinion of owners of the units. Majority of people feel that there is more strain on amenities in these complexes. At the same time a good number of people are satisfied with the amenities and have no complaints. Proper design and planning of the complex will reduce the strain. It should be considered while planning that how many units or how much of business is going to be accommodated in the building. Some people have expressed their anguish or not providing even toilet facilities in some of the complexes.

TABLE 5.12 : Hyderabad City: Opinion on Level of Amenities in High-Rise Commercial Complexes, 1991

Level of Amenities	No. of responses	Percent
Adequate	106	69.7
Not adequate	46	30.3
Total —	152	100.0

Source: Field work

Most of the owners of the commercial units in high-rise buildings are satisfied with their location in these buildings. But a sizeable percent of people want to shift their business from these buildings for varied reasons. This is particularly so with the units in buildings improperly maintained. Some of the shop-keepers are interested to shift their business to the larger units. Table 5.13 gives us the percentage of responses in shifting their units.

TABLE 5.13 : Hyderabad City: Percent Preference in Shifting the Shops/units from High-Rise Complexes, 1991

Opinion	No. of responses	Percent
Prefer to shift	30	19.7
Not prefer to shift	122	80.3
Total —	152	100.0

Source: Field work

Locating more number of units of different nature in a single building will boost the business. A customer wants to purchase his requirements at one place. If provisions are made for a variety of goods and services in a single premises it draws more customers from different places. Most of the respondents have agreed to the opinion that the high-rise buildings by their nature of large accommodation for varied shopping units will help in boosting the business.

A general perception on the commercial use of high-rise building space in Hyderabad city induces the developers to promote the real estate business in high-rise buildings. The business people will also look their new business in these eye catching skyscrapers. It is more appropriate to encourage commercial high-rise development in central areas which will reduce congestion and add to commercial and office space in CBD.

REFERENCES

1. Jean Gottmann, "Why the Skyscraper?", *The Geographical Review,* Vol. 56, No. 2, 1966, pp. 190-212.
2. J.B. Fleming, "An Analysis of Shops and Service Traders in Scottish Towns", *The Scottish Geographical Magazine,* Vol. 70, No. 3, 1954, pp. 97-106.
3. Raymond H.Elhs et al., (1981), *Tall Buildings in Central Business Districts: Management of Parking Needs,* Advances in Tall Buildings, CBS Publishers and Distributors, Delhi.
4. H.J. Gayler, "Social Class and Consumer Spatial Behaviour: Some Aspects of Variation in Shopping Patterns in Metropolitan Vancouver, Canada", *Institute of British Geographers Transactions,* Vol. 5, No. 4, 1980, pp. 427-445.
5. Richard V. Ratchiff, "Demand for Non-Residential Space", in *Readings in Urban Geography* (Ed.), The University of Chicago Press, Chicago, 1969.

6

LIVING IN HIGH-RISE BUILDINGS : PROBLEMS AND PROSPECTS

Living in high-rise building has become a common and growing phenomena in all over the World. There are number of cases in the West, where almost the entire urban population is housed in the multi-storeyed buildings (Madrid) and the residents appear to be satisfied with high-rise living.[1] In most of the cities of the developed countries, a large proportion of the urban population live in high-rise buildings.

The high-rise living has become most popular and acceptable in industrialized countries largely due to changes in household structure. The change from large, combined family to the contemporary nuclear family is the consequence of shift from agrarian to an industrial way of life. The households in general were reduced to smaller in size and required smaller living spaces. These smaller households prefer high-rise living because of its modernity, views, low maintenance costs and convenience. The living in high-rise has become an appropriate habitat for many modern city dwellers all over the World.

In Indian cities the high-rise residence is fast growing since last two decades. High-rise residential construction has become very popular in large cities. It can be presumed that the urbanization is an inducing factor for this urban phenomenon of high-rise living. The demands for space due to the pressure of urbanization in the inner cities has resulted in high-rise apartments to withstand the higher densities in these areas.

The development of high-rise residence depends upon the attitude of residents. High-rise living is mostly alienated and compartmentalized. This may put the residents into many social and psychological problems. These problems have to be identified and checked to make the living in high-rise more preferable and comfortable.

Here in this chapter an attempt has been made to examine the socio-economic conditions of the people living in high-rise residences in Hyderabad city and to analyse their social and psychological problems due to high-rise living.

Socio-Economic Conditions of the Households

Hyderabad city is known for its cosmopolitan character and is the confluence of many cultures. Its location and history made the people to settle here from different parts of the country. All religions and languages of India are found in this city. The people living in high-rise buildings also follow the traditions of Hyderabad culture by following the same cosmopolitan out look as in the case of general type of dwellings.

Religious and Linguistic Composition

Hyderabad city is a socio-cultural unit influenced by religious and linguistic factors. Like any other metropolis, Hyderabad displays a diversity of religious and linguistic groups. Though these groups are seggregated to some extent in the city, the composition in high-rise buildings is more or less same in all parts of the city. As seem from Table 6.1 the religious groups in high-rise buildings are largely influenced by the mix of different religious groups in the city as a whole (Fig. 6.1).

TABLE 6.1 : Hyderabad City: Distribution of Households in High-rise Buildings by Religion, 1991

(Percentage)

Religion	City zones			All Zones	Co-efficient of variability
	Hyderabad South	Hyderabad North	Secundrabad		
Hindus	40.9	77.8	77.0	74.9	17.63
Muslims	59.1	18.4	2.0	18.8	76.00
Christians	-	2.8	19.0	5.2	183.30
Others	-	1.0	2.0	1.1	260.00
All Groups	100.0	100.0	100.0	100.0	

Source: Field work

It is evident from the table that while the Muslims are forming a major proportion (59.1%) in Hyderabad South, the Christians are clustered to considerable proportion (19%) in Secunderabad area. The Hindus are the major religious group except in southern part where the high-rise development is insignificant. Muslims are negligible in Secunderabad area. Muslims, although form a large group of city population in high-rise living they are very few compared to other groups. This might be due to the fact that the Muslim population is clustered in south zone of the old city and the high-rise development is more towards North the Secunderabad.

A perceptive look at the values of co-efficient of variability among different religious groups shows tendencies towards agglomerative and

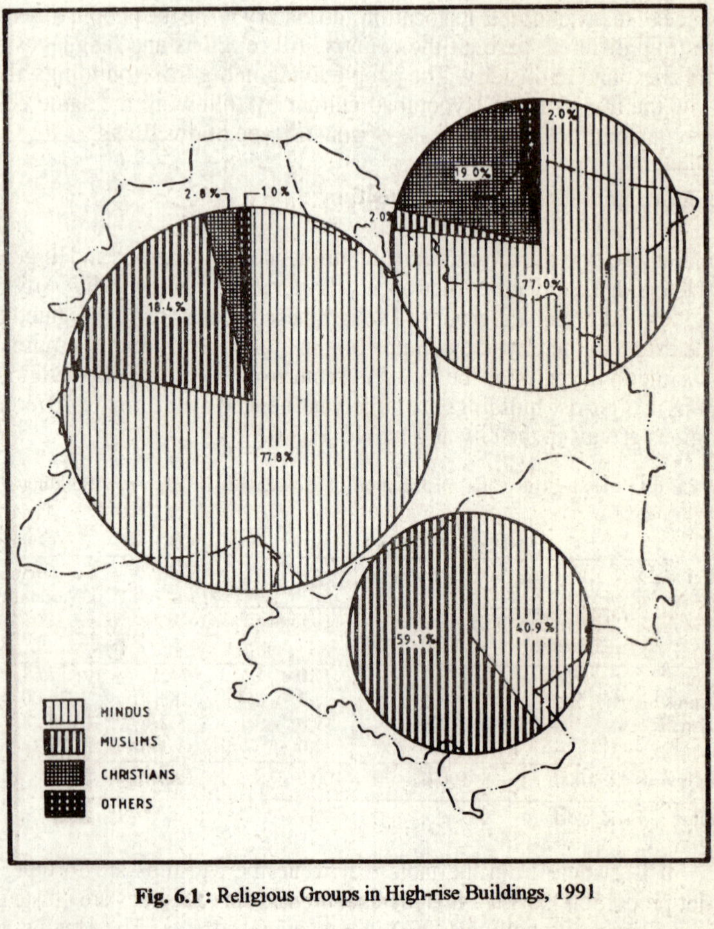

Fig. 6.1 : Religious Groups in High-rise Buildings, 1991

dispersive nature. The traditions, customs, attitudes etc. make the people following same religion or speaking the same language to cluster in distinct pockets. This tendency for social and cultural affinity pulls the like groups into more concentrations and finds the groups in spatial seggregation. Co-efficient of variability is an useful measure to find out the clustering or dispersive nature of different groups. It is a good statistical tool for observing consistency among variables. For Muslims, Christians and other groups a high co-efficient of variability is found which display a distinct inclination to cluster in pockets, whereas, Hindus as a category records relatively a low co-efficient of variability which shows a lesser inclination to cluster and hence seem to be more widely disseminated in the city fabric. Eventhough the high-rise living is not developed in all parts of the city to the same level the seggregation of these groups is distinct within the limited areas.

It is language which reveals better the nature of heterogenous and cosmopolitan character of the city. An analysis of linguistic composition of population gives a more representative picture of city's differing cultural associations. Among the residents of high-rise buildings all the different linguistic groups are found which the city contains in general, with varied proportions. Table 6.2 reveals the different per cents of the linguistic groups in high-rise buildings. Among all the groups Telugu speaking people are more. But an analysis of the groups by city zones reveals that Hyderabad South is predominantly Urdu speaking and in Secunderabad Sindhi, Hindi, Tamil, Gujarati and Marathi speaking groups are more compared to Telugu speaking groups which is quite contrary to the general population pattern in the city. This suggests that the well-to-do migrants from other States prefer high-rise living. Hyderabad North shows a more cosmopolitan nature by accommodating all linguistic groups in good proportion. If the Telugu and Urdu speaking groups are taken together still they account for less than half the population. This again suggests the preference of people from other states for high-rise living.

TABLE 6.2 : Hyderabad City: Distribution of Households in High-Rise Buildings by Languages, 1991

(Percentage)

Language	Hyderabad South	Hyderabad North	Secunderabad	All Zones	Co-efficient of variablilty
Hindi	9.10	15.66	16.66	15.44	58.03
Telugu	22.75	30.00	4.17	25.00	69.04
Urdu	54.55	17.05	2.10	17.42	77.53
Tamil	9.10	7.83	18.75	9.75	74.22
Sindhi	-	6.00	20.83	8.00	155.40
Gujarati	4.50	5.07	12.50	6.27	127.36
Marathi	-	5.53	6.25	5.23	143.02
Malayalam	-	2.30	4.17	2.45	154.92
Kannada	-	2.76	-	2.09	102.91
Others	-	7.80	14.57	8.35	78.12
Total	100.00	100.00	100.00	100.00	

Source: Field work

Co-efficient of Variability : $V = \frac{S.D.}{Mean} \times 100$

The clustering tendency (with high co-efficients of variability) is noticed among the Sindhi, Gujarati, Marathi, Malayalam and Kannada speaking people. The other linguistic groups although they record a moderate figures of co-efficient of variability the consistency is observed in all zones of the city (Fig. 6.2).

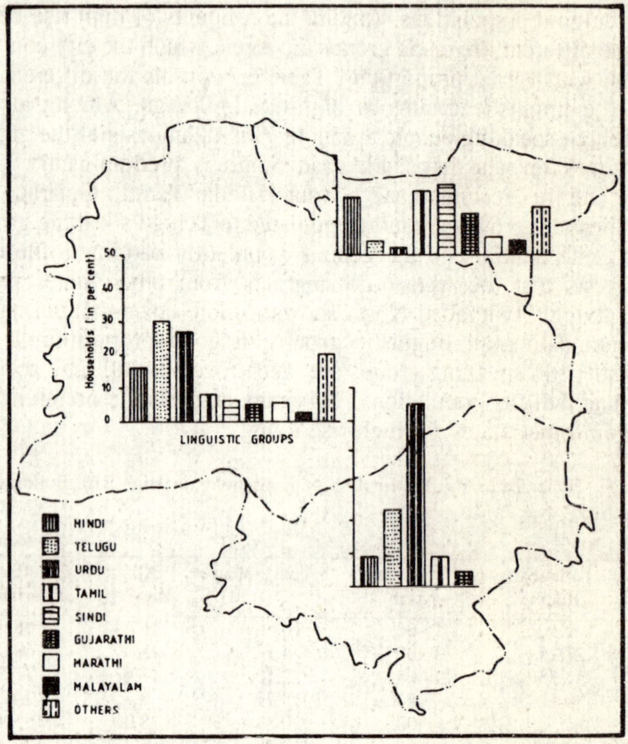

Fig. 6.2 : Linguistic Groups in High-rise Buildings, 1991

Age - Sex Compsition

Table 6.3 illustrates the proportion of different age groups of the people living in high-rise buildings in the city. Eight groups are shown for three different zones and city. More or less the structure of age groups for male and female are similar for all the zones. In the age group 50-59 a major

TABLE 6.3 : Hyderabad City: Residents of High-rise Buildings - Age-sex Ratio, 1991

Percentage

Age Group	Hyderabad South		Hyderabad North		Secunderabad		Total	
	Male	Female	Male	Female	Male	Female	Male	Female
0 - 14	12.75	10.78	9.31	8.23	13.08	8.38	10.25	8.50
15 - 19	4.90	4.90	7.28	5.73	6.81	5.76	7.00	5.66
20 - 24	6.86	3.92	3.94	3.46	5.24	2.62	4.42	3.36
25 - 29	3.92	5.88	4.42	5.25	1.57	2.62	3.90	4.86
30 - 39	6.86	8.82	5.49	7.40	4.19	7.33	5.40	7.52
40 - 49	8.82	9.80	11.34	10.50	14.66	13.08	11.67	10.88
50 - 59	4.90	1.0	9.07	3.46	6.28	1.05	8.22	2.83
60 and above	2.94	2.94	2.74	2.39	3.66	3.66	2.92	2.65
Total -	51.96	48.04	53.58	46.42	55.50	44.50	53.75	46.25

Source: Field work

disproportion of male and female ratio is noticed. The per cents of children and old age people are very less. It means the youth and middle age people are prefering more the high-rise living. If we observe the male female ratio, males (54%) are more than Females (46%) in all the zones (Fig. 6.3). But it is slightly less than the city's ratio (917 females per 1000 males). The parity of male and female populations reflects stable conditions of a society which may not always happen especially in metropolitan areas. The reason being the male population migrates to the cities first and after

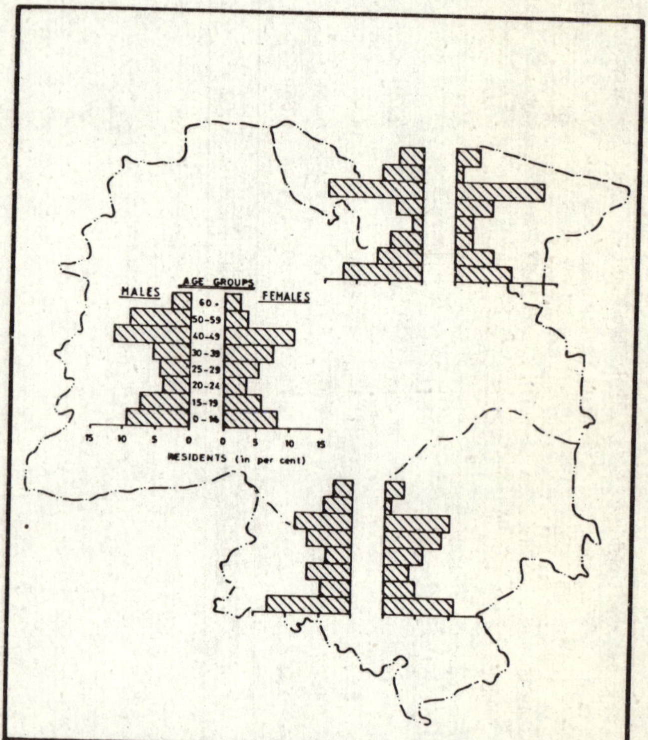

Fig. 6.3 : Age-sex Ratio of the Residents of High-rise Buildings, 1991

their stability female population move to the urban areas generally. This is a practical phenomena in most of the cities.

The average household size of the high-rise residents is slighlty less than four (3.94). The city's average household size according to 1981 census is 5.9. The household size is also an indicator of social development. Small size usually represents better social development. The household size of the high-rise residents is an indication of their social advancement and nature of family structure. The residents in high-rise buildings are predominantly small families, consisting of husband, wife and their few children.

Education and Occupation

Since the high-rise living is centrally located and has become a status symbol it is mostly prefered by the well educated people. It is found that cent per cent literacy is noticed among these residents and a careful look at the Table 6.4 reveals the level of education of the households. Educational level is high.rise as only one percent non-matric is found in Hyderabad North zone. Even the next category the matriculation are also negligible in other parts whereas in Hyderabad South it accounts for 13.6 per cent. The major proportion of people are graduates and they constitute above 60 per cent in all the zones. Except for South zone (18.2%), in remaining areas the University level of education is above 30 per cent (Fig. 6.4). With this one can infer that the high-rise living is preferred by well educated people.

TABLE 6.4 : Hyderabad City: Distribution of High-rise Residents Based on Education, 1991

(Percentage)

Education Level	City Zone			Total City
	Hyderabad South	Hyderabad North	Secunderabad	
Non-matric	-	1.0	-	0.7
Matric	13.6	4.1	6.3	5.2
Graduates	68.2	63.6	60.4	63.4
Post-graduates	18.2	31.3	33.3	30.7
Total -	100.0	100.0	100.0	100.0

Source: Field work

An analysis of the occupational structure of the residents would help to gain an understanding of their economic conditions and perhaps level of standard of living. Data on Table 6.5 clearly bring out the occupational structure of the residents of high-rise buildings in the city. Usually higher the level of education the status of occupation. Though technical and professional occupations are in considerable proportion in all the zones, it is businessmen

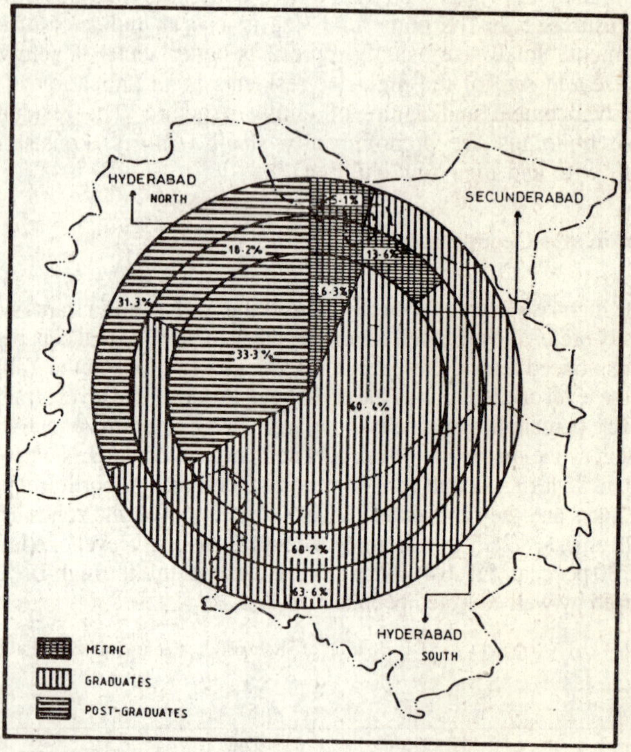

Fig. 6.4 : Distribution of High-rise Residents Based on Education, 1991

which accounts for above half of the households. In Secunderabad area it is 60 per cent (Fig. 6.5). This might be due to their preferential attitude to reside nearer to the work place. High-rise residential units serves the popular desire of the business people to live nearer to their business establishments. The lower level of occupation like clerical and others are very less in number.

Income

With a view to get further insight into the economic sturcture of the household in high-rise buildings in the city, the monthly income of the sample

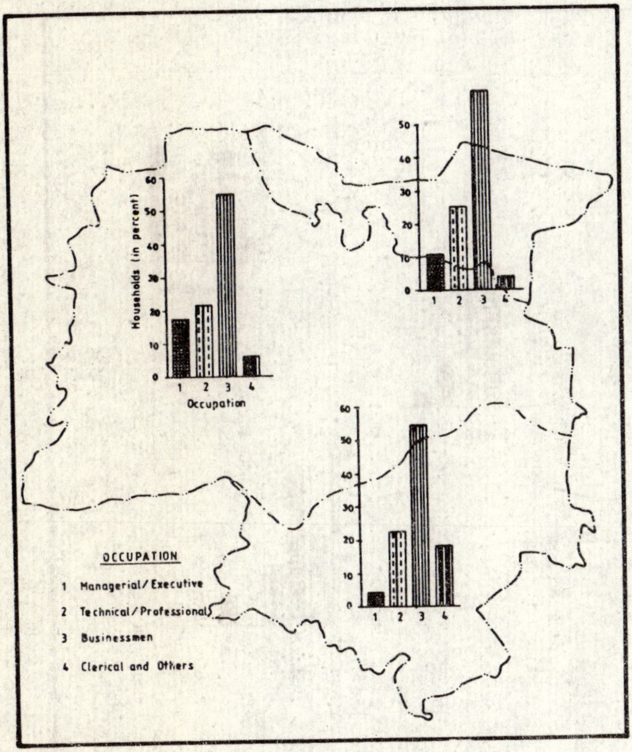

Fig. 6.5 : Distribution of High-rise Households by Occupation, 1991

TABLE 6.5 : Hyderabad City: Distribution of High-rise Households by Occupation, 1991

(Percentage)

Occupation	City Zone			Total City
	Hyderabad South	Hyderabad North	Secunderabad	
Managerial/Executive	4.5	17.5	10.4	15.3
Technical/Professional	22.8	21.7	25.0	22.3
Businessmen	54.5	54.8	60.4	55.8
Clerical and Others	18.2	6.0	4.2	6.6
Total -	100.0	100.0	100.0	100.0

Source: Field work

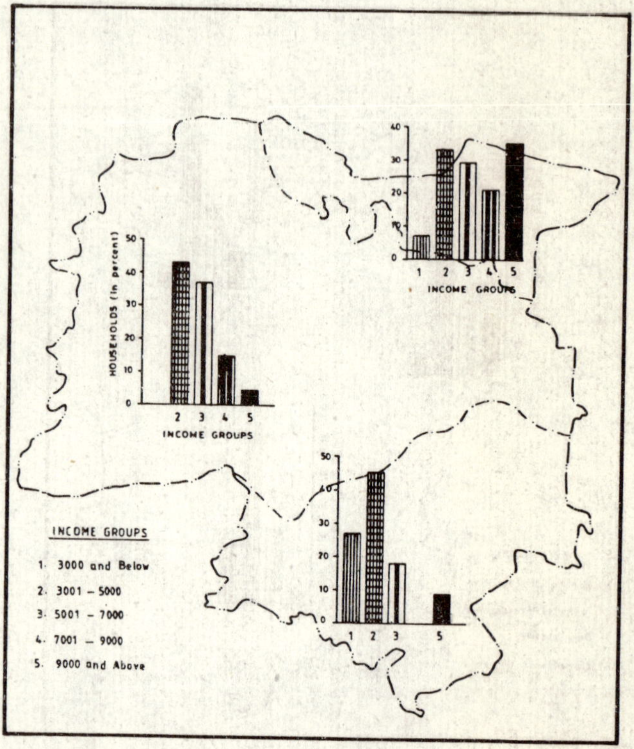

Fig. 6.6 : Distribution of Households in High-rise Buildings by Income Groups, 1991

households has been analysed (Table 6.6 and Fig. 6.6). It may be seen that the income group 3001-5000 accounts for a substantial proportion, 41.8 per cent of the households. There are very few in Secunderabad (6.3%) and a good proportion in Hyderabad South with the monthly income less than Rs. 3000. None of the households are below the monthly income of Rs. 3000 in Hyderabad North zone. The income group 5001-7000 accounts for 37.3 per cent in North zone where as households in this income range are less in other zones. In Secunderabad area the households with higher income above 9000 is substantially higher in proportion, 35.4 per cent, which is relatively more compared to other city zones. On an average it is noticed that the households in South zone are comparatively with low income and North zone and Secunderabad areas have more higher income groups. This may be due to the fact that the business people with higher income are more in these areas. As such it is a fact that the Hyderabad South is less developed presently.

TABLE 6.6 : Hyderabad City: Distribution of Households in High-rise Buildings by Income Groups, 1991

(Percentage)

Income (Monthly) Rs.	City Zones			Total City
	Hyderabad South	Hyderabad North	Secunderabad	
3000 and less	27.3	-	6.3	3.1
3001 - 5000	45.5	43.3	33.3	41.8
5001 - 7000	18.2	37.3	29.2	34.5
7001 - 9000	-	14.8	20.8	14.6
Above 9000	9:0	4.6	35.4	6.0
Total -	100.0	100.0	100.0	100.0

Source: Field work

High-rise building units, on account of their central location and high land value command very high rental value and consequently accessible only to the higher income groups who have the capacity to pay high rents. As the level of income of the high-rise residents is comparatively high, there seems to be hardly any difference in their life style and economic status. However, an analysis of their occpation reveals that a significant proportion of the residents are in occupations which generally provide relatively higher income (Table 6.7). It may be seen that over 55 per cent of the residents are engaged in business. The low income occupation, clerical/other jobs, accounts for just a little over 6 per cent of the residents. In other words the residents of high-rise buildings consist of highly educated professionals and businessmen whose income is relatively very high.

TABLE 6.7 : Hyderabad City: Distribution of High-rise Households By Income And Occupational Type, 1991

(Percentage)

Occupation Type	Monthly income (in Rs.)					Total
	3000 and less	3001-5000	5001-7000	7001-9000	Above 9000	
Managerial/ Executive	-	4.2	5.6	3.1	2.4	15.3
Technical/ Professional	-	8.4	10.1	3.1	0.7	22.3
Businessmen	3.1	24.1	17.8	8.4	2.4	55.8
Clerical/Others	-	5.2	1.1	-	0.3	6.6
Total -	3.1	41.9	34.6	14.6	5.8	100.0

Source: Field work

Work Place

In the choice of residential locations work place of the households plays a vital role. Work place residence relationship among the high-rise residents has been studied to gain an understanding of their daily movement and also to varify the fact that the households prefer the high-rise living because of proximity to their work place. Although the residential locations depends upon many factors like transportation costs, income, house rents, etc., the high-rise buildings because of their central location, are preferred for various reasons like less travel time, better transport facilities etc. Data on Table 6.8 clearly brings out the close relationships between work-place and residence of the residents of high-rise buildings. The general pattern is more or less the same for all the three city zones. Almost 60 per cent of the residents have their work place less than six kms. and a negligible of 6.9 per cent of them in Hyderabad North have their work place at a distance above 12 kms. It is significant to note that in the other two city zones none of the residents has work place above 12 kms. (Fig. 6.7).

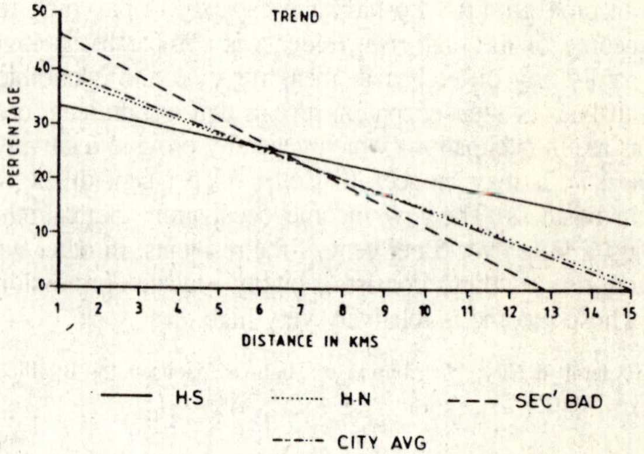

Fig. 6.7 : Work Place Residence Relationship : High-rise Residents (Zone-wise), 1991

It is observed from data on Table 6.8 that work place is one of the prime determinants of residential location for high-rise dwellers as more than 40 per cent households work within the radius of 3 kms. The proportion of households decline as the distance increases. But in Hyderabad South there is an increase in the distance between work place and residence. This is possibly due to the fact that the major

TALBE 6.8 : Hyderabad City: Work-place Residence Relationship of High-rise Residents by City Zones, 1991

(Percentage)

Distance from Work Place (in kms.)	City Zone			Total City
	Hyderabad South	Hyderabad North	Secunderabad	
1 - 3	40.9	40.1	43.8	40.8
4 - 6	18.2	20.7	25.0	21.3
7 - 9	13.6	25.4	27.1	8.0
10 - 12	27.3	6.9	4.1	8.0
Above 12	-	6.9	-	5.2
Total -	100.0	100.0	100.0	100.0

Source: Field work

work places in the city are located far away from this city zone. The major industrial areas, government offices and industrial and business establishments are all located far away in the northern parts of the city. Average distance travelled for work place by the high-rise household is found to be 5.5 kms. The businessmen activity has the least (4.1 kms.) and higher occupational categories like Managerial/Executive and Technical/Professional people travel greater distance for work (7.5 kms.). Therefore, the residential choice of the occupational types shows a highly dispersed pattern. Table 6.9 gives a clear picture of the work place distance based on occupational type for the different city zones (Fig. 6.8).

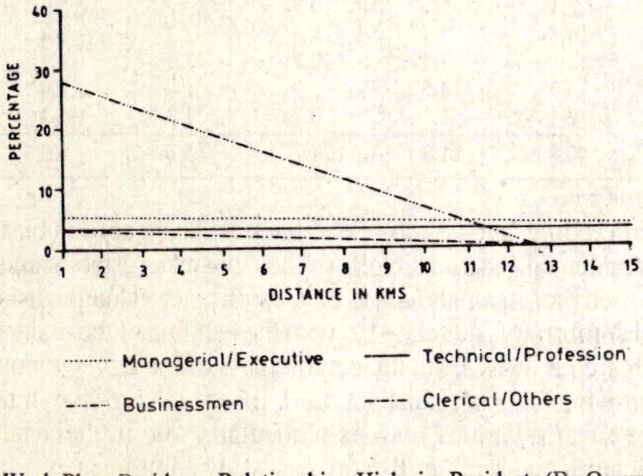

Fig. 6.8 : Work Place Residence Relationship : High-rise Residents (By Occupation), 1991

TABLE 6.9 : Hyderabad City: Work-place Residence Relationship of High-rise Residents by Occupational Type, 1991

(Percentage)

Distance from work place (in kms.)	Managerial/ Executive	Technical/ Professional	Businessmen	Clerical/ Others
1 - 3	1.1	0.7	35.5	3.5
4 - 6	2.4	7.0	11.5	0.3
7 - 9	9.1	10.5	2.4	2.8
10 - 12	2.1	3.8	2.1	-
Above 12	0.7	0.3	4.2	-
Total -	15.4	22.3	55.7	6.6
Average distance - travelled in kms.	7.8	7.5	4.1	4.7

Source: Field work

Income of the households has also a significant impact on the work place residence locations. Usually the high-rise residents belong to upper middle or higher income groups. Within them the low income group people tend to locate their residences near to the work place. The higher income group people, though travel long distances, want to locate their residences in high-rise buildings because of their central location. The data on Table 6.10 indicate that large proportion of the households with short distance work places are among the middle income group. However the households with long distance work places are also found to be substantial.

TABLE 6.10 : Hyderabad City: Work Place Residence Relationship of High-rise Residents By Income, 1991

(Percentage)

Monthly income (Rs.)	Distance from work place in kms.					Total
	1-3	4-6	7-9	10-12	>12	
Upto 3000	2.1	0.7	0.3	-	-	3.1
3001-5000	18.8	7.7	11.5	2.1	1.7	41.8
5001-7000	12.9	7.3	10.1	3.1	1.1	34.5
7001-9000	4.9	4.5	2.1	1.7	1.4	14.6
Above 9000	2.1	1.1	0.7	1.1	1.1	6.0
Total -	40.8	21.3	24.7	8.0	5.2	100.0

Source: Field work

From the proceeding analysis it is clear that people engaged in business tend to choose residential locations close to their business establishments while highly qualified professionals tend to have work place at longer distance. This pattern is in conformity and related to with the location of the major industrial areas which are far away from the central parts of the city. Obviously those professional while choosing distinct work places tend to live in the central parts of the city for various reasons particularly due to the availability of various amenities and services that are easily available.

Tenure Status

A house is one of the basic needs of man and the desire to own and live in one's own house is common. Usually one prefers to live in his own house rather than in a rented house. The proportion of owners and tenants will also help to understand the level of satisfaction in residential locations. The ownership of a residential high-rise flat in central city may be a form of investment with a view to earn a good return in the form of rents. So ownership of high-rise residential units may be for own use or for earning a regular income. The tenure status of the households in high-rise buildings is given in Table 6.11 (Fig. 6.9). It is observed that 60 per cent of the high-rise flats are owner occupied, and the remaining, 40 per cent are tenants. However the ownership pattern by city zones reveals some marked spatial difference. Hyderabad South is characterised by the lowest proportion of ownership (36%) while Hyderabad North has a corresponding figure of 63 per cent. In case of Secunderabad the ownership is just 52 per cent. Perhaps this ownership pattern has some relationship with economic dynamism of the various city zones. Hyderabad South is recognised on a decaying part of the city compared to the other city zones. Consequently most of the high-rise residential units on ownership basis are located in the more dynamic parts of the city i.e. Hyderabad North and Secunderabad.

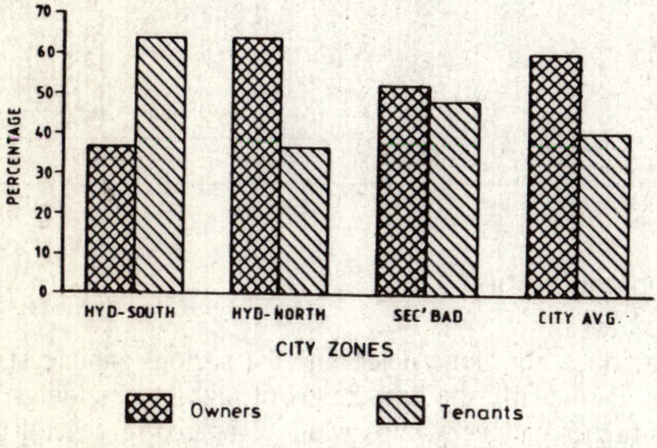

Fig. 6.9 : Tenure of High-rise Building Residents, 1991

TABLE 6.11 : Hyderabad City: Distribution of Households in High-rise Buildings By Tenure, 1991

(Percentage)

City Zone	Owners	Tenants
Hyderabad North	63.6	36.4
Hyderabad South	36.4	63.6
Secunderabad	52.0	48.0
Total city -	59.6	40.4

Source: Field work

The high-rise apartments due to their better location and high demand fetch the owner good rent. The rental value varies depending upon the size and area of the units. It is observed that there is not much difference in the sizes of the flats in the city high-rise buildings. Most of them are two or three bed room flats. But the difference in rent is noticed to be very high, depending upon the location and facilities provided. In Hyderabad south the rent of high-rise flats is below Rs. 2000 per month per residential units, whereas in North zone and Secunderabad areas a significant proportion of flats command much higher rent. Table 6.12 gives an insight into the rent pattern of high-rise flats in different city zones.

TABLE 6.12 : Hyderabad City: Distribution of Tenants in High-rise Buildings By Rents, 1991

(Percentage)

Monthly Rent (Rs.)	City Zones			Total City
	Hyderabad South	Hyderabad North	Secunderabad	
Below 1000	35.7	1.3	4.3	6.0
1000-1499	57.1	27.8	34.8	32.8
1500-1999	7.2	45.6	17.4	35.3
2000-2499	-	19.0	17.4	16.4
2500 & above	-	6.3	26.1	9.5
Total -	100.0	100.0	100.0	100.0

Source: Field work

Socio-Economic Status

The income does not alone determine the socio-economic status of the households. Particularly the households of high-rise buildings in the city belongs to higher income groups when compared to general population. Hence some other measures should be employed to examine the level and status of the households. The quality and level of goods and services used by the households can be considered as a good indicator of the standard of living.[2]

To obtain the standard of living or a comparative status, information on 13 variables ranging from air-conditioner to an electric fan has been collected from the sample households. Some of these economic variables are meant for necessities like motor car, scooter, etc. which serve transport needs of the households and others are meant for comforts such as washing machines, refrigerators etc. These variables have been ranked according to their perceived importance. The sum of the total ranks, given to these variables has been taken as a score and the maximum possible score for a household is 102. The maximum possible score has been multiplied by the total number of sample households in each city zone and this has been taken as unity. The actual total score for each city zone has been computed as a proportion of the maximum possible score for the zone.

$$\text{Standard score} = \frac{\text{Actual score}}{\text{Maximum possible score}}$$

The standard score of economic indicators used in the study ranges from zero to one. The higher the value of this score the higher level of living standard.

TABLE 6.13 : Hyderabad City: Socio-economic Status of Households in High-rise Buildings, 1991

City Zones	Maximum possible score	Actual score	Standard score of socio-economic status
Hyderabad South	2,244	1,289	0.57
Hyderabad North	22,134	15,145	0.68
Secunderabad	4,896	3,342	0.68
Total city	29,274	19,776	0.67
Co-efficient of variability			15.15

Source: Field work

It can be noticed from Table 6.13 that the overall picture of the city for high-rise households in terms of living standards is quite satisfactory. But on the same lines another study, has found that a very disheartening picture prevails for general population of the city (Gopi, K.N. and Kalpana, M., 1990). The standard score for high-rise residents at city level is 0.67. There is not much variation in the score among city zones, but Hyderabad South accounts for slightly less score of 0.57. The standard score also help in assessing the well-being of high-rise occupants. The co-efficient of variability for the standard score is calculated by examining the ward-wise information and is found to be 15.15, which reveals more consistency and uniformity in the status of the people in high-rise buildings.

Social Problems

People living in high-rise apartments have to face different type of environment, which is turn create specific problems for them. Different cultural attitudes towards density, space, privacy, security, social interaction, etc. of the individual and the family may result in varied problems as well as advantages. Usually the tall buildings are sometimes accused of being dehumanizing because they create 'compartmetalized' living and working spaces.[3] However, compartmentalized living is not unique to high-rise environments in the countries like India and other developing countries where people still live in close contact with nature and society. High-rise buildings seem to be approriate, especially as living spaces, for individuals affluent enough to leave them at will, independent enough to seek friends among strangers and autonomous enough to find pleasure and satisfying recreation in public spaces. But these buildings seem to be inappropriate for people whose economic conditions afford them little opportunity to get out of the house, who depend largely on the extended family or on the neighbourhood as an extension of family for their frienship and social contacts, and whose living patterns revolve around the security and familiarity of family-oriented private spaces.[4] The social success of tall buildings, though it depends upon income factors, seems to increase with a society's affluence, industrialization and individualization.

The social factors which are, one way or the other, responsible for the problems of the residents are so interwoven with man- environment relationships and cultural values. David Harvey observes that without an adequate understanding of social process. . . we cannot hope to understand social space in all its complexity.[5] Increasingly, therefore, attention is being paid to the causes of social environmental problems and the ways in which these various problems can be resolved. High-rise living which is associated with high density or overcrowding produces harmful social problems. For the present study, as the skyline of Hyderabad city has not yet reached the intensive problem level, the social problems faced by the high-rise residents are not so unbearable, as seen in the developed countries.

Social Alienation

A general complaint about high-rise living is social alienation, i.e. distance in personal relations. Personal distance - possibly the isolation usually depends upon culture as well as individual personality. But for many, one strong reservation about high-rise living centres is the sense of isolation the occupant feels. Amick and Kviz observe in their study that the social alienation increased with density and high per cent of alienation is found among the high-rise residents.[6] Social anonynity is one of the urban characertistics. This is more is high-rise living which leads to the alienation.

A mixed reaction is noticed when the people living in high-rise apartments are asked about their opinion on social alienation (Table 6.14). The level of alienation is found to be high in Hyderabad North and Secunderabad where the high-rise development is more. Due to the traditional mixup in the culture relatively less alienation is observed in Hyderabad South.

TABLE 6.14 : Hyderabad City: Opinion on Alienation Among High-rise Residents, 1991

City Zone	Total respondents	No. of positive responses	Percent
Hyderabad South	22	2	9.1
Hyderabad North	217	89	41.0
Secunderabad	48	21	43.8
Total City	287	112	39.0

Source: Field work

Essential Amenities

A high-rise building with many households is bound to have certain common amenities, in the absence of which the problems may arise for and among the households. Adequate parking space, proper vertical elevator system and good maintenance are all essential. The civic amenities like power and water supply, etc. have to be provided. The inadequacy and improper maintenance of these essential amenities will not only put the households into difficulties but also cause friction among the households.

The opinion of households on existing level of amenities in the high-rise residential units is documented in Table 6.15. Although the overall per cent of satisfaction on different amenities is above average, some of the households expressed their unhappiness as they have to face acute problems for these essential amenities. In one of the high-rise buildings located in the city centre water supply is very poor and the households are getting water daily by tanks on payment. For some households parking space is the major problem and there are instances the residents have to obtain parking space in nearby buildings at considerable inconvenience and cost. Poor design and poor maintenance is the chief cause for the inconvenience of the households. Yet another common complaint is the lack of adequate open space. This is particularly so in Hyderabad South and Secunderabad areas.

TABLE 6.15 : Hyderabad City: Level of Satisfaction of Residents on Amenities in High rise Residential Buildings, 1991

(Percentage)

Amenities	Hyderabad South	Hyderabad North	Secunderabad	Total city
Water supply	82.0	76.9	68.8	76.0
W.C.	72.7	91.2	95.8	90.5
Lift	54.5	71.9	83.3	72.5
Parking place	45.5	77.9	64.6	73.2
Open space	45.5	80.6	64.5	74.9

Source: Field work

Besides the above there are many problems which cannot be put into the empirical frame of analysis. The middle income extended family groups who spend a large part of their non-working time at home may not prefer the high-rise living due to the above problems.

Psychological Problems

It is often believed that the high-rise buildings are not good living environments because the residents feel imprisoned and isolated from people and other living things. Mental illness amoung high-rise flat dwellers, particularly women who live on upper floors and stay at home are more prone to loudiness, especially those who do not go out to work because of children.[7] The children are more likely to have psychological problems.[8] Some of the parents fear to send their children downstairs for playing. Inadequate play space may have some harmful effects on the health or intellectual development of very young children. Cappon[9] observes that the children in the high-rise structures are deprived of neighbourhood peers and certainly they are affected in their mental growth.

Physically unfit persons who must depend totally on mechanical transportation fear all the time that the elevator may fail and may cause mental tensions. It is usual that the lifts are not always dependable in high-rise buildings. This will create tension to the elderly residents also.

Though the attempt has not been made to get empirical data on the psychological effects of high-rise living, the author had the prevelege of discussion with the residents personally and they expressed the similar fears which have been discussed above.

The results of the earlier studies and the residents opinion conforms that high-rise living is psychologically fit for older people, childless couple and couples with grown children. However the author's observation is that the above situation is only partially valid for Hyderabad city conditions as the city high-rise buildings have not grown much and family ties in Indian homes are closely knit and have more attachments among the family members, which will reduce the mental tensions and psychological problems to some extent.

In spite of many social and psychological problems, high-rise living appears to be more satisfying. In certain circumstances high-rise buildings may be the only solution to urban growth. Where the geographic and political boundaries absolutely limit the possiblities for horizontal growth, while at the same time growing populations increase the demand for urban space, vertical growth by means of high-rise sturctures is found to be the only solution. High-rise buildings can also be made accessible to the lower income people with better planning. These buildings will reduce the burden on infrastructure of the city also to a considerable extent. With many positive aspects, high-rise living will have certainly more prospects in coming years in Indian cities.

Impact on the Sense of Well-Being

The effect of high-rise buildings on people's sense of well-being and their impact on the urban landscape is to be examined carefully as the high-rise phenomen on is growing rapidly in every croner of the urban World. The high-rise occupant's well-being is complex as the large number of people who occupy a high-rise building arc drawn from different social groups. First one has to define what is meant by well-being and what factors influence the level of human well-being. In the broader sense the well-being means the good or satisfactory conditions of existence.

In Hyderabad city, among high-rise residents there exists different cultures, religious and linguistic groups. The indicators of well-being of the high-rise occupants may differ from group to group. Hence a survey is conducted to collect their opinion on the level of satisfaction relating to their personal, housing and neighbourhood conditions. The informations collected through the survey has been processed by city zone and used in this study. The occupant's self reported satisfaction is referred to be a most appropriate measure of well-being. The emphasis on satisfaction derives largely out of concern to assess user needs. It is important to remember, however, that the information about whether an occupant is satisfied or not, does not necessarily provide a basis for implying what an individuals actual behaviour will be.

It is a general observation that the high-rise residential flats in Hyderabad city are accessible to above average income group people and the income level of the occupants is more or less in the higher income group.

As examined above (Table 6.13) their socio-economic status which was derived with the help of economic indicators such as Air-conditioner, Car, Refrigerator, etc. is also found to be satisfactory. These two measures also can be considered as the indicators of well-being. In addition these two, the level of satisfaction of residents on housing conditions is given in Table 6.16. Water supply, roads, recreation and parking facilities, are recorded for less satisfaction of the residents comparing to other indicators. Other than these four indicators the satisfaction level on housing conditions is above 90 per cent. The overall complex level of satisfaction for all the indicators put together for the city on housing conditions is 86.9 per cent which reveals the more satisfied condition of well-being of the high-rise residents.

TABLE 6.16 : Hyderabad City: The Level of Satisfaction of High-rise Residents on Housing Conditions, 1991

(Percentage)

Housing Condition	Hyderabad South	Hyderabad North	Secunderabad	Total city
Location	100.0	98.0	100.0	98.6
Accommodation	95.5	98.0	100.0	98.5
Neighbourhood	95.5	98.0	100.0	98.5
Sanitary facilities	90.1	91.2	98.0	92.3
Water supply	77.2	75.6	89.6	78.0
Roads	54.5	65.4	81.3	67.2
Public Transportation	81.8	88.9	93.8	89.2
Shopping facilities	90.9	94.5	91.7	93.7
Recreational facilities	68.2	66.8	68.8	67.2
Educational facilities	95.5	96.3	91.7	95.5
Health facilities	95.5	96.3	93.8	96.2
Parking facilities	77.3	66.8	68.8	67.9
Index of satisfaction	85.6	86.4	89.8	86.9

Source: Field work

Safety and Security

In addition to satisfactory level of amenities, the occupant's safety in high-rise buildings also draws considerable attention. The condition relating to the safety and security in the building have direct impact on the sense of well-being of the occupants. Therefore, suitable standard have to be adopted in designing and planning of building to safeguard against threats of safety such as earthquakes, fire accidents, etc. Proper attention has to be paid with regard to security for controlling all sorts of crimes and thefts, etc. Occupants in the high-rise buildings in Hyderabad city have expressed their satisfaction on the safety and security measures. Most of the buildings are strictly maintained with security guards. But it is personally noticed that in many buildings there are lapses on following the fire hazards preventive measures. It is also observed that the most of the flats are handed over to the owners by the developers without getting a clearance certificate from the Director of Fire Services which is compulsory for high-rise buildings.

Physical and Social Disadvantages

The immediate surrounding area of the high-rise building i.e. the neighbourhood also affect the well-being of the occupants. Actual response of the occupants has been obtained on different variables relating to the neighbourhood, which will help us in assessing their well-being. Under the physical disadvantages, traffic, noise, unpleasant odours, dirt and dust, maintenance of the roads and drainage, etc. have been included to obtain the level of dissatisfaction of the residents. Social disadvantages also have been assessed by taking the opinion of residents on density of population, heterogencity of castes, different income groups, civic consciousness and domestic help, etc.

A common measure to assess the level of disadvantages to the residents has been obtained by dividing the actual number of responses to the listed disadvantages with the total number of possible responses of households.

$$\text{Level of Disadvantage} = \frac{\text{Actual No. of responses of all listed disadvantages}}{\text{Total positive responses}} \times 100$$

Thus obtained figures are listed in the Table 6.17. An analysis of the table bring out the variations in level of disadvantages as perceived by the households in different city zones. Interestingly it is noted that the level of physical disadvantages (51.3) is more than the level of social disadvantages which is found to be 40.1 for all zones.

TABLE 6.17 : Hyderabad City: Level of Disadvantages of Neighbourhood For High-rise Residents, 1991

Disadvantages	City Zones			All zones
	Hyderabad South	Hyderabad North	Secunderabad	
Physical disadvantage	46.2	51.5	52.4	51.3
Social disadvantage	34.0	41.8	35.0	40.1

Source: Field work

The well-being of the occupants, which is a perceptive measure, cannot be assessed in its totality. In different circumstances it varies from time to time. However, it must be emphasised that all the above factors have varying influence over the residents of high-rise buildings.

Besides the varied opinion of residents on different issues and their differing cultures, a general harmony among the residents is evident in all areas of the city. The above analysis of the household profile and their responses will help the planner to design well suited and problem free high-rise apartments.

REFERENCES

1. Lynn S. Beedle (Ed.), Council on Tall Buildings, Group PC, 1981, *Planning and Environmental Criteria for Tall Buildings*, ASCE, New York.
2. Gopi, K.N. and Kalpana, M., *Energy, Environment and Human Well-being: An Urban Perspective*, Concept Publishing House, New Delhi, 1992.
3. Cooperman, *Social Research and Tall Habitats*, 1977.
4. *Ibid.*
5. David Harvey, *Social Justice and the Cities*, Edward Arnold Ltd., London, 1973.
6. Amick, D.J., and Kviz, F.J., 'Social Alienation in Public Housing: The Effects of Density and building Types', *Ekistics*, No. 231, Feb. 1975, pp. 118-120.
7. Adams and Conway, *'Some Social Implications of High-rise Housing'*, 1974.
8. Gregoire, M., 'The Child in High-rise', *Ekistics*, No. 186, 1971, pp.331-33.
9. Cappon, D., 'Mental Health in High-rise', *Ekistics*, No. 196, 1972, pp.192-95.

7

SOCIO-ECONOMIC IMPLICATIONS OF HIGH-RISE REDEVELOPMENT

High-rise development in Indian cities is certainly a part of the redevelopment process. Initially the cities tend to grow horizontally and in the process the central parts become old and dense. As the space requirements in the central parts becomes acute, vertical expansion takes place by renovating, altering and dismantling the old buildings. The available open spaces will be absorbed by the high-rise structures due to the steep rise in land values. Though the cities in India are absorbing sorrounding land to a large extent in their growth process, high-rise building construction usually occurs in and around the main business district, not in the newly developed outer areas.

The development of high-rise building construction is influenced by several factors such, as the age of city, the availability of open spaces, wide roads and transportation facilities, and the customs and habits of the people of the region. The building regulations of the local civic bodies also play a vital role in the development of high-rise structures.

In Hyderabad city the high-rise development is in the process since last two decades with marked intensive growth for the last five to six years. This has been caused by the ever increasing demand for both commercial and residential space due to the large influxes of population into urban areas. Being the state capital and its cosmopolitan culture it set a new trend to absorb the high-rise building structures in the central parts of the city, by replacing old traditional buildings and absorbing open spaces. With the creation of more vertical living and commercial space in these areas, more morphological and functional changes have been taking place. The high-rise redevelopment causes many social and economic implications. It is the people who make the city more prosperous. The development and change in the social and physical fabric of the city is intended to meet their increasing needs.

Infrastructural Facilities

The development of high-rise project is not an issue involving the design of a single building. Rather it is a process of neibhourhood development and aimed at designing and planning of a community since it serves the needs of groups of people. Therefore, provision of adequate services and infrastructural facilities are integral part of the project and any short-coming in this regard would be a serious lapse. For budget-reduction purposes, many facilities may be dropped or the level of facilities may be kept low leading to serious problems.

A clear distinction has to be made between a facility and a service. A facility is space or area provided for an activity such as play area, parking place, or a laundry room, etc. A service on the other hand is provided by a service deliverer and may not require specific space or area. Therefore, the user requirements have to be assessed properly and to be taken care of while planning and designing the whole project. High-rise buildings should not be considered in isolation, they have to be examined as part of the whole neighbourhood. An intensive high-rise development may cause the changes in existing system of the urban services and infrastructure in the city.

There is a differing opinion among the residents regarding the facilities in the high-rise buildings. Perhaps due to lack of wider open spaces, it is noticed that, no high-rise complex in the city has provided the play space for children which considered to be a compulsive facility for the cultivation of good mental health among the children. The more caged and closed door life will certainly cause to develop the isolated nature among them. But interestingly it is observed that many of the parents are not aware of the seriousness of the problem and are not much concerned about the lack of play space in the complex. However, it is found that in most of the buildings some common space is provided for security guard, office room of the residents association etc. Local authorities should insist on the provision of minimum compulsory facilities within the building which may give the residents more satisfied habitat.

In Hyderabad city the high-rise development is sporadic and wide spread. Mostly, they have been constructed as single blocks. This might be the reason for not providing much open spaces in the neighbourhood. In most of Indian cities redevelopment is not planned for entire neighbourhood at a time. The process is taking place on its own spontaneously. Therefore, planners have to insist this gradual change to suit the integral plan of the neighbourhood. The setting of high-rise building within the infrastructure of neighbourhood is essential. Presently the high-rise buildings are coming up as a process of redevelopment within the developed neighbourhoods which already has a community of people living or working there. Therefore, the existing services and infrastructure will have a direct influence on this new type of development. The way of fitting of this new development into the social and infrastructural network of the neighbourhood may cause either positive or negative effects on both.

The viability of high-rise buildings depends on the adequacy of urban services and infrastructure of the neighbourhood and city as a whole. Urban services are those functions that serve the city - they serve the people who live there and those who visit. These services are either functional which include things like transportation, water supply, sanitation systems, delivery of food and other services, and fire protection, etc. or social which include welfare, education, recreation, health and the like. On one hand the functional services give the city life and maintain it, on the other social services play a vital role in the social and cultural viability of a city. Beedle[1] observes that the entire physical system that makes possible the delivery of these services is the infrastructure of the city. This infrastructure system is more important in the consideration of high-rise development.

Usually the high-rise development will reduce the length of infrastructural network by lessening the cost. Since the high-rise development is in the inner parts of the city there won't be much expenditure on providing the infrastructure to these buildings. In comparison the suburbs which are caused by city growth, cost more expenditure on providing these services at considerable distances. High density may have a direct relation with the strain on the infrastructure. But it is observed that in Hyderabad the areas with high-rise development are recording much lower densities than the other areas in many parts of the city. Of course, in future, the problem may arise if necessary corrective steps for provision of infrastructure facilities at appropriate level are not taken.

It is evident from the earlier studies that high-rise buildings make possible an economic use of municipal services and infrastructure through developing higher densities. The study on *The costs of Sprawl* (1974)[2] reveals that for streets and roads, utilities. . . the high-rise apartments is less expensive. The total operating cost for 1000 high-rise (6-8 storey) apartments would be 32 per cent of 1000 conventional single-family houses, the greatest savings being in streets and roads. However, Correa and Lamela observes that if, within an existing urban infrastructure, increases net density results in increased demand or need for local urban services which are not adequate to the task, then the costs to the city for providing roads, water supply and sewer, as well as mass transportation must be taken into account.

In a city like Hyderabad, which is just beginning to construct high-rise buildings in large numbers, it is most important that these buildings be carefully integrated into the urban plan if the costs for utilities and transportation to be maintained at lesser level than horizontal expansion. If the planning and construction of tall buildings are not carefully coordinated with those of the urban infrastructure, the municipal costs of transportation, utilities and other services may go up, which in turn affect the long-range urban economics.

The situation did not arise so far in the areas of high-rise buildings in the city to feel the burden on the services and infrastructure of the locality as well as on the whole city. The large proportion of dwellers favour the existing high-rise situation in the context of neighbourhood facilities (Table 7.1). A large proportion of high-rise dwellers in all the three zones have expressed their satisfaction on the urban services and infrastructural facilities.

TABLE 7.1 : Hyderabad City: Level of Satisfaction of High-rise Dwellers on Urban Services and Infrastructure, 1991

City Zone		Percent Satisfied	Percent Unsatisfied
Hyderabad South		85.6	14.4
Hyderabad North		86.4	13.6
Secunderabad		89.8	10.2
City Average	—	86.9	13.1

Source: Field work

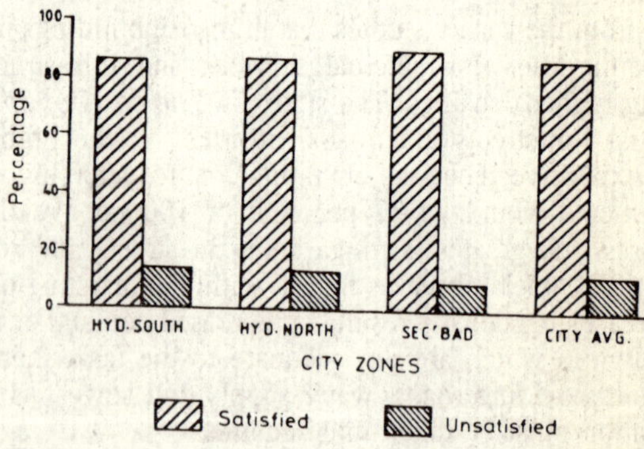

Fig. 7.1 : Level of Satisfaction on Urban Services and Infrastructure, 1991

The development of high-rise buildings can either aggrevate problems of traffic congestion, open spaces and strain on civic amenities etc. or perhaps be part of the solution. High-rise buildings could be more acceptable in some situations than a smaller ones. The location of the buildings in the absorbable areas will result positive effects. Hyderabad North and Secunderabad zones are capable of absorbing more high-rise buildings where as Hyderabad South, the old city may not favour the high-rise trend due to its high density and conservative, traditional and cultural reasons. As such the existing pattern of high-rise development in city also conforms to the varying nature of the city zones.

Parking Needs

One of the major implications of high-rise redevelopment in central parts of the city is parking needs. Usually high-rise buildings irrespective of their use represent major concentrations of human activity and generate more trips of public movement. Usually in this areas the movement of people is by means of vehicles which result in the need for parking space. Studies proved that the trip generation by auto trips is more with tall building developments (Richard J.Hocking).[3] The local agencies have to carefully examine the need and see that the enough parking space is provided for each new development so as not to be a burden on the city's transportation and parking system.

Many of the high-rise dwellers and shop-keepers have expressed their dissatisfaction on the existing parking place for high-rise buildings (Table 7.2). The problem is accute in the central parts of Hyderabad and Secunderabad during office hours. It is important that local governments take steps for effective management of existing parking space as well as provision of additional space wherever possible and necessary.

TABLE 7.2 : Hyderabad City: Level of Dissatisfaction on Parking Facilities, 1991

(Percentage)

City Zone	Percent of Dissatisfaction	
	Residential Units	Commerical Units
Hyderabad South	22.7	73.3
Hyderabad North	33.2	50.5
Secunderabad	31.3	73.8
City Average —	32.0	59.2

Source: Field work

Economic and Social Implications

High-rise buildings can be the lowest cost solution. Where the cost of urban land is high, the land cost per unit will be much less in case of high-rise apartments in comparison to the low- rise units on the same land. The optimum height or the trade-off level in high-rise construction varies from place to place depending upon the relative costs of available resources and materials. High investment in high-rise development is necessary for reasons of structural safety and for the provision of essential mechanical and electrical services such as lifts, elevators and fire safety devices etc. Usually with the increase of height the cost of construction also goes up. The operation and maintenance cost of these buildings will also increase. Therefore, the height of buildings must fully take advantage of the permissible FAR to obtain an optimum cost effectiveness.

There is differing opinion on the escalation of land values due to high-rise development and quite a few feel that "the accumulation of large population in small areas leads to skyrocketing land values and to the economic necessity of high-rise buildings" (Solvadori, 1974).[4] The other view is that "major antisocial contribution of high-rise buildings is to the spiralling up of land prices" (Gokhale, 1974). Both are based on the circular phenomenon that high land value causes more intensive land use with more vertical space by means of high-rise construction, which is turn bring land values to a still higher value and so on (Contini, 1973).[6] The two opposite interpretations of this phenomenon begin at different points of the same circle.

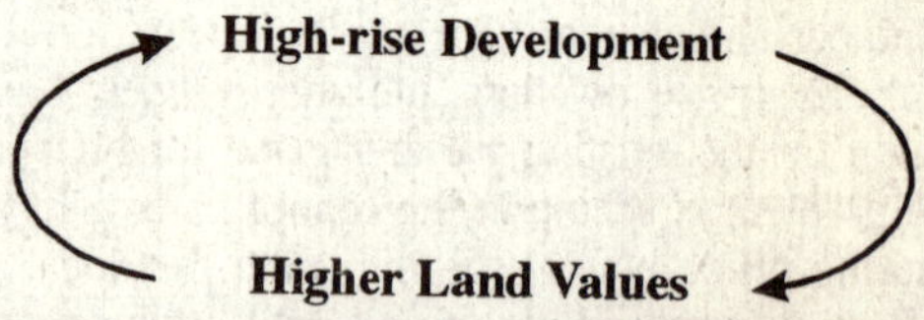

Due to high land values and high construction cost the accommodation in high-rise buildings become expensive. Only high income families can afford to purchase the flats in high-rise buildings. In Hyderabad city also the high-rise building space is in the reach of upper middle class and higher income group thus depriving the residential space for poor and lower income people.

On the other hand, the high initial investment of capital in high-rise development, affects the interests of small builders in their business. High-rise building projects have developed a monopolistic situation, because of their higher costs where only those few real estate operators having sufficient financial resources can stay in the field.

However, in Hyderabad city the cost of high-rise building space has not yet reached higher level comparable to other metropolitan cities. Still it is within the range of Rs. 300-450 per sq.ft. depending upon location. As such the height of the buildings are also at moderate level.

By observing the present trend, it can be assumed that the present trade off point for high-rise construction may be 8-10 floors in the city.

High-rise redevelopment causes the change in the social fabric of the neighbourhood also and leads to certain social implications in the stream of the existing social form. The high-rise complexes bring large concentrations of people to the central and selected areas of the city which create stress on the existing sociophysical fabric. In Hyderabad city, the high-rise development is wide spread with mostly one or two blocks. The concentration is not as dense as in the case of developed countries where the social strains are found to be high. In most of the areas there are single dwelling units all around the high-rise complexes and consequently the neighbourhood system remain more or less un-affected. However, a micro-scopic view of the social fabric within these high-rise complexes gives a different picture in their social form.

High-rise living tends to encourage the break-up of large family groups into a small nuclear family consisting of the couple and their one or two children. It may create some panic among the extended family societies like ours. More social alienations and less human binding forces among the family members may result with their compartmentalised living. There is also more possibility of an increased risk of individual occupants suffering from some one else's negligence simply because the number of occupants of the building is high. Crime and vandalism too are potential dangers in these buildings. In the study on *The costs of Sprawl*[7] it is postulated that a 20 per cent increase in crime in the high density planned community over the low density. Socio-economic conditions and inappropriate high-rise design can both aggravate the conditions of high density. However, Adams[8] argues that the vandalism and crime are not caused by high-rise housing, but its design appears to facilitate their occurrence.

It has been ascertained from the residents of high-rise dwellings in the city as to how they feel about safety, security and crime in the high-rise complexes. Most of them have expressed their satisfaction on these issues. it might be, perhaps, due to the fact that these buildings have not been much detached with the adjacent neighbourhood. Some of the social disadvantages which are incroporated in the Table 7.3 are the resultant implications of high-rise redevelopment. However, the intensity of these disadvantages have not been felt much in any zone of the city. Unit being treated as the maximum level of disadvantage, each type of disadvantage has been examined in isolation.

Impact of Development Process of city

As a city expands, the changes that high-rise buildings bring about in the skyline may be symbolic of the growth and development of the urban area.

TABLE 7.3 : Hyderabad City: The Level of Intensity of Social Disadvantages for High-rise Dwellers, 1991

Social Disadvantage	Level of Social Disadvantage			Total City
	Hyderabad South	Hyderabad North	Secundra-bad	
High Density of Population	0.41	0.43	0.27	0.40
Heterogeneity of castes	0.09	0.14	0.08	0.12
Different income groups	0.05	0.07		0.05
Inadequate civic consciousness	0.59	0.58	0.39	0.55
Shifting of people		0.05	0.04	0.04
Non-availability of Domestic help	0.82	0.82	0.88	0.83
Social Alienation	0.09	0.41	0.44	0.39

Source: Field work

Contini feels that high-rise structures can have specific urban value as landmarks and points of reference as definers of "nodes", "edges", or "gateways" of cities.[9] Some cities derive their character specifically from tall buildings and New York is an example.

If a city derives its character or image largely from historical sturctures, the problem of introducing modern high-rise buildings is a delicate one. Hyderabad city, despite of its historical conservative movement, shows a duel character for both old and new trends.

High-rise buildings can either lead or follow the development or redevelopment pattern of an urban area. Based on the demand of space, more vertical residential and commercial space is created by redeveloping the urban cores. Available open spaces in the inner parts are also subjected to this process. Hyderabad city derived its skyline mostly due to the revitalization of the central parts in North zone and Secunderabad areas.

The city benefits from the concentration of business space and business activity that high-rise development generates. In most cities, high-rise have evolved in concentrations in central areas of cities and at other locations that are highly attractive, and those concentrations generate the highest tax returns to local government. For example in Chicago, approximately one-third of the city's real estate tax return comes from the greater downtown area covering less than 7 per cent of the total area of the city (Beedle).

It is observed in most of the cases that high-rise buildings and the uses that occupy them usually return more revenue to local governments than they require in services (costs) from them. This positive cost-benefit ratio is often used as a measure of the attractiveness of a development.

High-rise structures also influence the city form and organization. Burgess (1925) and Homer Hoyt (1939), who analysed American Cities and Society, and propounded their theories on the city's form, noted that the patterns of city growth and evolution formed 'rings' around the denser central or downtown area with certain understandable variations.[10] The centre zone of the city and the zones of variation subsequently became the locations of most of the high-rise development and contributed a significant portion of the city's land value and tax revenue.

In Hyderabad, for historical and culturual reasons, the high-rise development does not exhibit the form of rings. However, the central area is concentrated with denser high-rise development and spread into pockets in other places of economic importance.

It is clear that the high-rise building has been and will continue to be a strong urban influence. Their contribution and impact on the city's development is undoubtedly very high. On the other hand, they may also cause adverse effects, if they are badly placed or designed without sensitivity.

REFERENCES

1. Lynn S. Beedle, *Urban Services and the Infrastructure, in Advances in Tall Buildings*, CBS Publishers and Distributors, Delhi, 1984.
2. Real Estate Research Corporation, *The Costs of Sprawl*, New York, 1974.
3. Richard J. Hocking, *Shared Parking considerations of Tall Buildings*, in *Advances in Tall Buildings*, CBS Publishers and Distributors, Delhi.
4. Solvador, M.G., 1974.
5. Gokhale, R.G., 1974.
6. Contini, E., (1975), *Tall Buildings: Urban Planning Factors.*
7. *Ibid.*
8. Adams (1974). *Some Social Implications of High-rise Buildings.*
9. *Ibid.*
10. Park, R.E., Burges, E.W. and Mckenzie, R.D., *The Growth of City: An Introduction to a Research Project in the city*, University of Chicago Press, Chicago.

8

SUMMARY AND CONCLUSION

Cities tend to change their structural pattern in the central and other parts of economic importance to suit the growing needs of both commercial and residential purposes. The old structures under go change and leads to displacement with new buildings usually the modern trend of high-rise structures which provide more space to live and work. The remodelling or redevelopment of the existing old structures is a growing phenomenon in the cities of developing countries.

Urban redevelopment which comes within the scope of the renewal concept is used to describe as any replacement of old structures with new ones. It is also concerned with rehabilitation or development of open spaces as in the case of dead or arrested sub-divisions where no demolition of any kind is involved, redevelopment should be based upon the most appropriate landuse for the area as established by comprehensive city plan. Unfortunately, in Indian cities the redevelopment process is taking place in a sporadic and piecemeal basis that too mostly in the central parts of the city, where intensive landuse is found. A successful redevelopment programme can be carried out only where all the properties subject to redevelopment are assembled under one ownership and developed within the framework of comprehensive plan of city. Unplanned development may sometimes accrue benefits and also strains to the surroundings. The result of redevelopment of an area is the rise in revenues from taxes and lowered costs of functional services and infrastructure of the city. The real advantage of the programme is raising of social and physical standards in the neighbourhood. It also gives a new lease of improved economic life to the city.

The redevelopment of the inner city areas is closely related to the vertical growth of the city. The increased demand for commercial and residential use in the areas of high land values generate the high-rise structures to accommodate more business and living space with more financial returns. High-rise development as a result of redevelopment process brings an increased and more active life to the areas, which induce the adjacent areas also to under go morphological changes.

Slowly it grows not only vertically but also horizontally in the form of sprawls into the surrounding areas.

The city of Hyderabad is the fifth largest metropolitan city of India, with a population of about 4.1 million (1991). After the formation of Andhra Pradesh, the city experienced tremendous growth of population which resulted not only peripheral growth, but also an intensification of residential and commercial activities in the city core. The changes in the skyline of the city have been taking place during last two decades to provide more working and living space to the large influx of migrants. Particularly the central parts of the city have undergone drastic changes by following the modern trend of high-rise phenomenon. A large number of multi-storeyed residential apartments and commercial complexes have sprung up in and around the central city.

High-rise Process and Trends

Every city has a core and usually growth takes place concentrically around the core. But Hyderabad, due to historical and varied cultural reasons, has developed two urban cores, around which the city has grown. Three distinct areas with differing characteristics exist in the city are Hyderabad South (the old city), Hyderabad North (the new city of Hyderabad) and Secunderabad. Though the high-rise trend exists in these three zones, the latter two experience considerably more intense development, as their central parts are the location of nuclei. Though the Hyderabad South is historically old and need much redevelopment, the shift in the residential growth and economic activity towards North Hyderabad has caused more concentration of vertical dimension in North Hyderabad. Secunderabad, with its own core area, allows the process at equal rate. The areas along main routes joining these two urban cores are absorbing more high-rise structures both commercial and residential complexes. The location of more government institutions and offices in these areas are also playing as an inducing factor for the high-rise development.

The city skyline has not even reached the mark of 20 floors so far. The building with fifteen floors is the highest and naturally it belongs to the commercial high-rise as the case everywhere. Usually commercial buildings are taller in any city. The average high-rise constructions in the city are observed to be about 8-10 floors.

The emergence of high-rise trend in the city is after 1970. Prior to this new housing complexes were single, ground plus one or two storey buildings. But during the last decade housing under private sector in the inner city was mostly in the form of high-rise apartments. In the recent years high-rise dwelling has become very popular in this city.

The commercial high-rise is growing up within and around the CBDs in Hyderabad and Secunderabad. Most of the complexes adjacent to main roads are used for mixed purpose. Usually the ground and first floors are being used by small commercial units, shops and the upper floors are for residential purpose. High-rise buildings for institutional purpose are very few and mostly they are located in Hyderabad North.

Keeping in view the saturated densities and more strain on services and infrastructure, restrictions are imposed by the government by issuing the multi-storeyed regulations to prevent further growth in certain areas. The haphazard growth of the high-rise buildings may lead to many social and civic problems if the local bodies do not insist on strict regulations. Municipal Corporation and HUDA are showing keen interest in this aspect.

The Building Process

The process of vertical development includes the hardware systems—the building process and software as well-the marketing and management techniques. In Hyderabad city it is a general observation that the high-rise building projects are mostly the part of redevelopment or urban renewal programmes. In most of the cases in the inner cities the high-rise projects are the resultants of demolition.

The Building activity in Hyderabad city is in the hands of both private and public agencies. High-rise building is mostly promoted by the private builders. This building industry is providing employment directly or indirectly to many qualified, skilled and unskilled persons. The main objectives of the real estate business in this line might be the profit oriented, but it is engaged in catering the sapce demand for dwelling and commercial use in the central parts of the city.

The investment pattern in high-rise buildings is varied and on average the total cost of the project is shared initially by the purchasers, developers and financing agencies. The financial institutions are assisting in the promotion of these projects. The demand for the high-rise space in the city is found to be moderate and satisfactory. The demand is varied with the site location.

The marketing of the high-rise units is not in a difficult stage. Apart from the developers themselves the agents are assisting in the business for its promotion. The role of the real estate agents in the high-rise building business appears to be like salesmen for the housing industry and to generate effect very similar to that of advertising.

The builders feel that the finance is the major problem faced by them in the process in addition to many other like building material, land acquisition, labour and marketing, etc. Though the many new builders are coming forward to solve the accute shortage of residential units in the city, very few are staying in the business for longer period. The difficulties in the system are forcing them to withdraw from the business. It is required to find out the reasons and the nature of difficulties in the system and to persuade them with the intervention of authorities for the better promotion of housing industry by means of vertical growth. For example, the existing zoning regulations, building acts and regulations, corporate stipulations have to be examined carefully. It is also opined by many people that the present FSI allowed in the city is very low compared to other cities which can be increased for the central parts of the city.

Commercial and Business Use

High-rise building space is most important from the commercial point of view. With the rise in the intensity of commercial and business space in the central parts and other developed places of economic importance in the city, the creation of more vertical space takes place. The increase in commercial and business space in these areas is due to the process of redevelopment. Urban redevelopment device is a method of accelerating the natural readjustments of landuse patterns.

A close examination in the spatial pattern of commercial space use in high-rise buildings indicates that the commercial high-rise development has been taking place around the two commercial cores of the city, Abids and Secunderabad. It is also observed that the Basheerbagh area has the capacity to absorb more commercial high-rise buildings. The distribution of shopping units have been examined according to the size of the units based on their floor space (carpet area) and their annual turn over. Though the smaller units are found more in number the percent carpet area under larger size units amounts to be more. Annual turnover of the equal size units in Secunderabad is relatively higher than Hyderabad North and Hyderabad South. There is no direct relationship between carpet area of the shop and their annual turnover. The overall spatial commercial high-rise space use exhibits a concentration of both the retail and wholesale commercial activity.

The tenure and rent pattern is examined for the high-rise commercial space and it is noted that about 87 per cent of the shop-keepers or owners of business establishments in these units are tenants. The average rent per square foot carpet area varies with the size of the unit and its location. The rent per unit area is found to be relatively more for the smaller size of units. Secunderabad shows more economic dynamism by its intensity of commercial activity in the commercial high-rise buildings.

It is also observed that the high-rise structures are not planned to the full satisfaction of commercial space users. More complaints have been noticed regard to varied problems like parking place, maintenance amenities and location, etc. Since the problems have been looked into with the view of space users they ought to be given more attention in future.

High-rise Living

High-rise living has become more acceptable with the reduction in family size in modern way of life. The households in general were reduced to smaller in size and required smaller living spaces. These smaller households prefer high-rise living because of its modernity, location, views, low maintenance costs and convenience, etc. Urbanisation is the inducing factor to adopt this new trend of modern living style. The average household size of the high-rise residents in Hyderabad city is found to be four.

In Hyderabad city the people living in high-rise buildings closely follow the traditions of Hyderabad culture by exhibiting the same cosmopolitan outlook as in the case of general type of dwellings for which the city is known as the confluence of many cultures. The religious and lingusitic composition of the people living in high-rise buildings reflects this cosmopolitan character of the city to the satisfaction of the reader. Though the Hindus as a category shows a lesser inclination to cluster and widely disseminated in the city fabric the minority groups such as Muslims, Christians and other groups display a distinct inclination to cluster in pockets. The linguistic composition of population gives a more representative picture of city's differing cultural associations. Among all Telugu speaking people are more. In Hyderabad South, Urdu speaking group is a major proportion compared to others.

The families residing in high-rise buildings are consisting the larger proportions of youth and middle age groups. The children and old age people are comparatively less. Much difference is not noticed in the male and female ratio with few exceptions. Majority of the dwellers belong to a nuclear family of middle aged wife and husband with one or two grown up children.

The educational level of the high-rise residents is high and cent percent literacy is noticed among these residents. The status of occupation is also to be found high, with a considerable proportion of technical and professional occupations. Businessmen accounts for about half of the households whose income range is above average. It is clearly noticed that the high-rise residents belong to the upper middle income group or higher income groups. It is evident from the analysis of income groups that the high-rise dwellings is not in the reach of lower income people. Within the available income groups Hyderabad South contains the households with low income thus exhibiting its backwardness of relatively less development compared to other zones.

Usually, the households prefer the high-rise living because of proximity to their work place. It is observed that a little more than half of the residents have their work place within the distance of less than six kilometers. Again it is the businessmen who travel less distances for their work places. However, the technical and professional people are known for travelling longer distances for work. On the whole the residential choice of the different occupational types shows a highly dispersed pattern.

The major occupancy of the high-rise dwellings in the city is by owners. The tenants are less in number except in Hyderabad South zone where the rental value is found to be very less comparing to other parts of the city.

The socio-economic status of the high-rise residents is found to be quite satisfactory. Their living standard is found to be above average which indicates the well-being of the occupants. The well-being has been perceived as the good or satisfactory conditions of existence. The occupant's self reported satisfaction on their personal, housing and neighbourhood conditions is found to be above average despite some dissatisfaction prevail on certain issues. The overall complex level of satisfaction for different indicators put together for the city on high-rise living is about 87 per cent which shows more satisfied condition of well-being of these residents and could be taken as their approval for high-rise living.

The residents of the high-rise buildings have to face a different type of environment, and due to different cultural attitudes towards density, space, privacy, security and social interaction etc. of the individual and the family may result in varied problems. It is observed that a mixed and variety of social and psychological problems are experienced by the high-rise dwellers in the city. These are caused chiefly due to the poor planning aspects of these buildings. But these are not yet at an unbearable stage as seen in the developed countries. The level of satisfaction of the residents on amenities in high-rise residential buildings is quite good and it supports the assumption of low problem level in these buildings. The fact is that the skyline of Hyderabad city has not yet reached the intensive problem level. No doubt, the response of the residents regarding physical and social disadvantages is noticed to be of considerable level, but the level of satisfaction on housing conditions reveal their approval for the high-rise dwelling in the city. Whatever may be the varied opinion of the residents on different issues because of their differing cultures, a general harmony among the high-rise residents is evident in all areas of the city.

Implications of High-rise Redevelopment

The development of high-rise buildings is influenced by several factors. In addition to the dismantling of old buildings, the available open spaces are absorbed by the high-rise structures due to the steep-rise in land values, resulting more morphological and functional changes.

The city benefits from the concentration of business space and business activity generated by high-rise development, which also increases the tax revenue of local government. It is observed that land values have reached the peak in the areas of high-rise development which are interlinked with each other.

High-rise development will reduce the length of infrastructural net work. In Hyderabad the high-rise construction is within the developed inner parts of the city and does not exert any pressure on the existing service and infrastructure system so far. But there is possibility of straining the physical fabric with further intensive concentrations of high-rise structures. The study reveals that the people are satisfied to large extent by the existing facilities except for parking needs. It is noted that parking especially for commercial complexes is inadequate and intervention of local authorities is essential to solve the problem.

Since the high-rise development in the city is in infant stage and not yet reached to dominate the traditional type of living, its impact on the social life is not much. However, some of the disadvantages are noticed with this new modern trend of urban form.

Keeping in view the present situation and emerging trend of high-rise development in the city the following suggestions are made with a view to encourage high-rise development more attractive in the context of the overall development process of the city.

1. High-rise development should be encouraged in the areas of higher demand upto the attainment of optimum landuse.
2. Public awareness programmes be introduced to mobilise public and private resources for capital investment and for maintenance support.
3. Proper implementation of multi-storeyed building regulations with least political intervention.

4. Promotion of organised real estate agencies/developers of high-rise projects.
5. Before high-rise buildings are allowed to be put up the adequacy of water supply, sewerage, power supply etc. should be ensured. Also the requirements as regards roads, traffic, parking, open spaces, etc. should be planned well in advance.
6. Fire-safety aspects should be considered right from the construction stage of high-rise buildings with particular reference to services and fire fighting aspects.
7. Inspection schedules should be established with specific guidelines as to assess the adequacy and strain on the infrastructural facilities.
8. The infrastructure maintenance and high-rise development should be tied to the comprehensive planning programme of the city.
9. The problem of viability of high-rise buildings should be studied not in isolation but in totality including social and long-term costs.

BIBLIOGRAPHY

Abler, R., Adams, J.S. and Gould, D.R., *Spatial Organisation: The Geographers View of the World*, Engle Wood Cliffs, Prentice Hall, New Jersey, 1972.

Adams, B. and Conway, J., *Some Social Implications of High-rise Housing*, New york, 1974.

Ahmed, F.M. and Frank, J.Costa, "All Jarudiyah: A Model for Low-rise/High Density Development in Saudi Arabia", *Ekistics*, Vol. 48, No. 287, 1981.

Alam, S.M., *Hyderabad-Secunderabad:A study in Urban Geography*, Allied Publishers Pvt. Ltd., Bombay, 1965.

Alam, S.M., "Vulnerability and Resilience of Cities: The case of Hyderabad", UNESCO Pilot Project Report, Centre for Area Studies, Osmania University, Hyderabad (Memeo).

Alam, S.M. and Khan, W., *Metropolitan Hyderabad and its Regions: A strategy for Development*, Asia Publishing House, Bombay, 1972.

Anas Alex, "Dynamics of Residential Growth", *Journal of Urban Economics*, Vol. 5, 1978.

Alonso, W., "A Theory of the Urban Land Market", *Papers and Proceedings of the Regional Science Association*, Vol. 6, 1960, pp.149-158.

Andrew M.Kirby, "Housing Market Studies: A Critical Review", *Institute of British Geographers Transactions*, Vol. 1, No. 1, 1976, pp. 2-8.

Ball, M. and Kirwan, M., "Accessibility and Supply Constraints in the Urban Housing Market", *Urban Studies*, Vol. 14, No.1, 1976.

Berry, B.J.L. and Horlon, F.E. (Eds.), *Geographic Perspectives on Urban Systems*, Prentice Hall, New Jersey, 1970.

Bhoosan, B.S., Mahadev, P.D. and Singh, J.P., "Shelter in an Urban Village: A case study from Mysore, India", *Ekistics*, Vol. 48 No. 287, 1981.

Boddy, M.J., "The Structure of Mortgage Finance, Building Societies and the British Social Formation", *I.B.G. Transactions*, Vol. 1, No. 1, 1976, pp.58-71.

Bookes, J.A. and Hughes, K., "Housing Redevelopment and Rehabilitation: A case study in Comparative Economics", *Town Planning Review*, Vol. 46 1975, pp. 215-225.

Bourne, L.S. (Ed.), *Internal Structure of the City-Readings on Space and Environment*, Oxford University Press, London, 1971.

Boyce, K.R., "Changing Pattern of Urban Land Economics", *Professional Geographer*, Vol. 15, 1963.

Brooks, Edwin, "Spatial and Social Constraints in the Inner City", *Geographical Journal*, Royal Georaphical Society, Vol. 141, Nov. 1975.

Cappon, D., "Mental Health in the High-rise", *Ekistics*, No. 196, 1972, pp.192-95.

Carter, Harold, *The Study of Urbán Geography*, Arnold Heinemann Publishers, New Delhi, 1979.

Carter, R.R. and Others, Area Improvement Policies for Inner City, Coventry The Project, London, 1972.

Chary, T.M.V. and Reddy, K.N., "Urban Housing: Housing Needs of Hyderabad City", in *Urban Crisis in India* (Ed.), Hyderabad Publishers, Hyderabad, 1985.

Chorley, J. Richard, et al. (Ed.), *Socio-economic Models in Geography*, Ethuen, London, 1967.

Clarke, M. and Wilson, A.G., "The Dynamics of Urban Spatial Structure: Progress and Problems", *Journal of Regional Science*, Vol. 23, No. 1, 1983.

Coleman Woodbury, *Urban Redevelopment: Problems and Practices* The University of Chicago Press, Chicago, 1962.

Cooperman, D., *Social Research and Tall Habitat*, New York, 1977.

Council on Tall Buildings, Group PC 1981, Planning and Environmental Criteria for Tall Buildings, Volume PC of Monograph on Planning and Design of tall Buildings, ASCE, Yew York.

Countini, E., *Tall Buildings: Urban Planning Factors*, New York, 1973.

Cropper, M.L., "The Value of Urban Amenities", *Journal of Regional science*, Vol. 21, No. 3, 1981.

Dan Soen, "Habitability - Occupants Needs and Dwelling Satisfaction", *Ekistics*, Vol. 46, No. 275, 1979.

Dan Soen and Ora Agnon, "The Human Mix in Neighbourhoods: Some Preliminary Conclusions", *Ekistics*, Vol. 47, No. 216, 1973.

Daniel Cappon, ."Mental Health in the High-rise", *Ekistics*, Vol. 196, 1972, pp.192-95.

David A.Kirby, *Slum Housing and Residential Renewal: The Case in Urban Britain*, Longman Group Ltd., London, 1979.

David Harvey, *Social Justice and the City*, Edward Arnold Ltd., London, 1973.

Davis, Otto, A., and Others, The Shrinkage in the Stock of Low- quality Housing in the central city: An Empirical study of the U.S. Experience over the last ten years", *Urban Studies*, Vol. 11, 1974, pp. 13-26.

Desai, A., "The Environmental Perception of an Urban Landscape: The case of Ahmedabad", *Ekistics*, No. 283, pp. 279-85.

Donald H.Webster, *Urban Planning and Municipal Public Policy*, Harper & Bros. Publishers, New York, 1958.

Donald, G. Jud and James Frew, "Real Estate Brokers, Housing Prices and the Demand for Housing", *Urban Studies*, Vol. 23, No. 1, 1986.

Donna, Duvall, "The Differential Effects of Apartments and Single Homes on Woman with Young Children", *Ekistics*, Vol. 48, No. 287, 1981.

Dumbleton, R. and Others, "Redevelopment in Two City Centres, *Town and Country Planning*, Vol. 42, Feb. 1974.

Duncan, S.S., "Research Directions in Social Geography: Housing Opportunities and Constraints", *I.B.G. Transactions*, Vol. 1, No. 1, 1976, pp. 10-19.

Elgie, R.A., "The Seggregation of Socio-economic groups in Urban Areas: A Comment", *Urban Studies*, Vol. 16, 1979.

Fleming, J.B., "An Analysis of Shops and Service Trades in Scottish Towns", *Scottish Geographical Magazine*, Vol. 70, No. 3, 1954, pp. 97-106.

Foreman Peck, J.S. and Grip Alos, P.A., "Inner City Problems and Inner city Policies", *Regional Studies*, Vol. II, No. 6, 1977.

Galanty, E.Y., "Housing Policy and Settlement Planning as Instruments of Social Stability in South-East Asia", *Ekistics*, Vol. 49, No. 292, 1982.

Ganz, Alexander, "The Future of the central city", *American city*, Vol. 85, August 1970.

Garg, S.C., "Strategy for Housing the Poor in Bhopal, India: A study of Squatters", *Ekistics*, Vol. 48, No. 286, 1981.

Gary Eldred, *Real Estate Analysis and Strategy*, Harper & Row Publishers, New York, 1987.

Gayler, H.J., "Social Class and Consumer Spatial Behaviour: Some Aspects of Variation in Shopping Patterns in Metropolitan Vancouver, Canada", *I.B.G. Transactions*, Vol. 5, No. 4, 1980.

George Simpson and Fritz, Kafka, *Basic Statistics*, Oxford & IBH Publishing Co., New Delhi, 1971.

Gerda Wekerle and Edward Hall, "High-rise Living: Can the Same Design Serve Young and Old", *Ekistics*, No. 196, 1972.

Gibbs, J.P. (Ed.), *Urban Research Methods*, Van Nostrand Co. Inc., New Jersey, 1961.

Goodchild, Barry, "Class Differences in Environmental Perception: An Exploratory Study", *Urban Studies*, Vol. 11, 1974, pp. 157-168.

Gopi, K.N., *Urban Growth and Industrial Locations*, Oxford and IBH Publishers, New Delhi, 1980.

Gopi, K.N. and Kalpana, M., *Energy, Environment and Human Well-being : An Urban Perspective*, Concept Publishing House, New Delhi, 1992.

Gottileb, M., "Influence of value in urban Land Market, 1956- 61", *Journal of Regional Science*, 1965.

Gottman, J. "Why the Skyscraper?", *Geographical Review*, Vol. 56, No. 2, 1966, pp.190-212.

Graham Davies, "An Economatric Analysis of Residential Amenity", *Urban Studies*, Vol. 11, 1974.

Gregoire, M., "The Child in the High-rise", *Ekistics*, No. 186, 1971, pp. 331-33.

Gruen, V., *The Heart of our Cities : The Urban Crisis : Diagnosis and Cure*, Thames and Hudson, London, 1965.

Hamzah Sendut, "Town Planning and Community Restructuring in Malaysia", *Ekistics*, Vol. 49, No. 292, 1982.

Hancock, Tom (Ed.), *Growth and Change in the Future City Region*, Leonard Hill, London, 1976.

Jackson, J.N., *The Urban Future: A choice between Alternatives*, Allen & Unwin, London, 1972.

James Q. Wilson, *The Record and the Controversy*, The MIT Press, Massachusetts Institute of Techology, Cambridge, Massachusetts, 1964.

James, B.K. and Sirmans, C.F., "The Demand for Urban Residential Land", *Journal of Regional Science*, Vol. 27, 1982.

Jane Darke and Roy Darke, *Who Needs Housing*?, The Macmillan Press Ltd., London, 1979.

Jewel Bellush and Murray, H., *Urban Renewal: People, Politics and Planning*, Doubleday and Co., Inc., New York, 1967.

John F. McDonald, *Economic Analysis of an Urban Housing Market*, Academic Press, New York, 1979.

Johnston, R.J., *City and Society, Unwin Hyman Ltd., London, 1989.*

Jones, C. (Ed.), *Urban Deprivation and the Inner city*, Croom Helm, London, 1979.

Kevin R.Cox, Man, *Location and Behaviour: An Introduction to Human Geography*, John Wiley and Sons, Inc., New York, 1972.

Kulkarni, K.M., *Geography of Crowding and Human Response*, Concept Publishing Co., New Delhi, 1984.

Leslie Martin and Lionel March (Ed.), *Urban Space and Structure*, Cambridge University Press, London, 1975.

Lin Thaiker, "Design for Better Living Conditions in Singaporc Flats", *Ekistics*, Vol. 40, No. 238, 1975.

Lottman, Herbert, R., *How cities are Saved*, Universe Books, New York, 1976.

Lynn S.Beedle, "Urban Services and the Infrastructure", in *Advances in Tall Building*, CBS Publishers & Distributors, Delhi, 1981.

Madhava Rao, A.G. et. al. (Ed.), *Modern Trends in Housing in Developing Countries*, Oxford & IBH Publishing Co., New Delhi, 1984.

Mark Dynarski, "Residential Attachment and Housing Demand", *Urban Studies*, Vol. 23, No. 1, 1986.

Mathur, G.C., "Impact of High-rise Development on Land values in India", in *Advances in Tall Buildings*, CBS Publishers and Distributors, Delhi, 1981.

Medhurst, D.F. and Lewis, J.P., *Urban Decay: An Analysis and Policy*, Macmillan, London, 1969.

Mehta, B. Jaswant, *High-rise Buildings*, M/s. Skyline, Bombay, 1978.

Misra, R.P. (Ed.), *Million Cities of India*, Vikas Publishing House, New Delhi, 1978.

Modak, N.V. and Ambedkar, V.N., *Town and Country Planning and Housing*, Orient Longman Ltd., Bombay, 1971.

Mohammad, Noor, *Slum Culture and Deviant Behaviour* Idarah-i-Adabiyat-i-Delhi, Delhi, 1983.

Muth, R., "The Derived Demand for Urban Residential Land", *Urban Studies*, Vol. 8, 1971.

Muth, R., *Cities and Housing: Chicago Unviersity Press*, Chicago, 1969.

Muttalib, M.A., *Urban Renewal: A case study for the old city of Hyderabad*, Regional Centre for Urban and Environmental Studies, Hyderabad.

Park, R.E., Burges, E.W. and Mackenzie, R.D., "The Growth of city: An introduction to a research project, in *The City*, University of Chicago Press, Chicago.

Patrick, I.Warkely, et al., *Urban Housing Strategies*, Pitman Publishing Ltd, New York, 1976.

Paul Lawless, *Britain's Inner Cities - Problems and Policies*, Harper & Row Publishers, London, 1981.

Peter Hagget, *Locational Analysis in Human Geography*, Edward Arnold, London, 1966.

Pocock, D. and Hudson, R., *Images of the Urban Environment,* Macmillan, London, 1978.

Ramachandran, H., "Residents' Perception of Living conditions in Bangalore, India", *Ekistics,* Vol. 52, No. 312, 1975.

Rangwala, S.C., *Town Planning,* Charotar Publishing House, Anand, 1987.

Ravindra Prasad D., (Ed.), *Urban Renewal: The India Experience,* Sterling Publishers Pvt. Ltd., New Delhi, 1989.

Real Estate Research Corporation, *The Costs of Urban Sprawl,* New York, 1974.

Richard J. Hocking, "Shared Parking Considerations of Tall Buildings", in *Advances in Tall Buildings,* CBS Publishers and Distributors, Delhi, 1981.

Robert C. Williamson, "Socialization in the High-rise: A cross-national comparison", *Ekistics,* Vol. 45, No. 268, 1978.

Robert K.Home, *Inner city Regeneration,* E & F.N. Spon, London, 1982.

Robert C.Weaver, *The Urban Complex,* Doubleday & Company, Inc., New York, 1964.

Robson, Brian, T., *Urban Social Areas, Theory and Practice in Geo graphy Series,* Oxford University Press, London, 1975.

Samuel Paul, *Apartments - Their Design and Development,* Reinhold Publishing Corporation, New York, 1967.

Satish Sinha, *Slum Eradication and Urban Renewal: Patna,* Inter-India Publications, New Delhi, 1985.

Scott Greer, *Urban Renewal and Amercian Cities,* The Bobbs - Merill Co., Inc., New York, 1981.

Sharma, R.S., *Urban Decay in India,* Munshiram Manoharlal Publishers Pvt. Ltd., New Delhi, 1987.

Short, J.R. and Bassett, K.A., Housing Policy and the Inner city in the 1970s", *I.B.G. Transactions,* Vol. 6, No. 3,1981.

Silkim, John, "New Towns and the Inner City", *Town and Country Planning,* Vol. 44, September 1976.

Sinha, M.M.P., *The Impact of Urbanisation on Landuse in the Rural-Urban Fringe,* Concept Publishing Company, New Delhi, 1980.

Smith, D.D., *Urbanization, Housing and the Development Process,* Croom Helm, London, 1981.

Stewart, John, "The Inner city challenge", *Municipal Review,* Vol. 45, July 1974.

Stuart, F. Chapin Jr., *Urban Land Landuse Planning,* Harper and Bros., New York, 1957.

Taylor, P.J., *Quantitative methods in Geography: An Introduction to Spatial Analysis,* Houghton Mifflin, Boston, 1977.

Teo Siew Eng, "Residential choice in Public and Private Housing in Singapore", *Ekistics*, Vol. 45, No. 270, 1978.

Toyne, P. and Newby P.T., *Techniques in Human Geography*, Macmillan, London, 1976.

UNESCO, *Conservation of cities*, Croom Helm, London, 1975.

Vithal Reddy, K. and Ram Mohan Rao, R. (Ed.), *Urban Crisis in India*, Hyderabad Publishers, Hyderabad, 1985.

Vijaya Bhole, *Housing and Urban Development in India*, Classical Publishing Co., New Delhi, 1988.

Vishwanadham, G., *Urban Demography and Ecology: A case study of an Indian city (Hyderabad)*, Life and Light Publishers New Delhi, 1979.

Ward, Pamela (Ed.), *Conservation and Development in Historic Towns and Cities*, Oriel Press, 1968.

Wayne Simpson, "Workplace location, Residential location and Urban commuting", *Urban Studies*, Vol. 24, No. 2, 1987.

Werner Z. Hirsch, *Urban Economic Analysis*, Tata McGraw- Hill Publishing Co., Ltd., New Delhi, 1975.

Whitehand, J.W.R., "The study of variations in the Building Fabric of Town centres: Procedural Problems and Preliminary findings in Southern Scotland", *I.B.G. Transactions*, Vol. 4, No. 4, 1979.

Whitehand, J.W.R., "Building cycles and the spatial pattern of Urban Growth", *I.B.G. transactions*, No. 56, 1972.

William, P., "Building societies and the inner city", *I.B.G. Transactions*, Vol. 3, No. 1, 1978.

Williams, P.R., "The Role of Institutions in the Inner London Housing Market: The case of Islington", *I.B.G. Transactions*, Vol. 1, No. 1, 1976.

William S.W. Lim., "Tall Buildings for Urban Centres in Third World Countries", *Ekistics*, Vol. 40, No. 238, 1975.

William Lim, *Equity and Urban Environment in the Third World, New Art Printing* Co., Pvt. Ltd., Singapore, 1975.

Yadav, C.S., *Landuse in Big Cities: A study of Delhi*, Inter-India Publications, Delhi, 1979.

REPORTS AND GOVERNMENT PUBLICATIONS

Director of Town Planning, Development Plan for Hyderabad City (Vol. I and II), Government of Andhra Pradesh, Hyderabad.

Health, Housing and Municipal Administration Department, 'Development Plan for the area comprising the Municipal Corporation of Hyderabad', Government of Andhra Pradesh, Hyderabad, 1975.

Housing, Urban Rnewal and Ecology Board (in collaboration with Bombay Housing and Area Development Board), 'Feasibility Report on Urban Renewal Scheme for Kamatipura', BMRDA, Bombay, July, 1981.

The Indian Institute of Economics, Study on Optimal Metropolitan Development of Hyderabad, Hyderabad, 1979.

Town and Country Planning Organisation, Redevelopment of Shahjahanabad-The Walled City of Delhi, (Resume of the Seminar and Background papers), Ministry of Works and Housing, Government of India, New Delhi, 1975.

Multi-storied Buildings Act, 1981, Hyderabad Urban Development Authority, Hyderabad.

National Building Code of India, 1983, Indian Standards Institution, Government of India, New Delhi.

Census of India, Series 2, Andhra Pradesh, Part II-A, General Population Tables 1971 and 1981, New Delhi.

Census of India, Series 2, Andhra Pradesh, Part VI-A, Town Directory, 1981, New Delhi.

Census of India, Series 2, Andhra Pradesh, Part XIII-A and B, Village and Town Directory, Village and Town Primary Census Abstract, Hyderabad, 1981.

INDEX